R CRAIG CAMPBELL

THE HOME UNIVERSITY LIBRARY
OF MODERN KNOWLEDGE
242

THE ECONOMICS OF MONEY

The Economics of Money

A. C. L. DAY

LONDON
OXFORD UNIVERSITY PRESS
NEW YORK TORONTO

Oxford University Press, Amen House, London E.C.4

GLASGOW NEW YORK TORONTO MELBOURNE WELLINGTON
BOMBAY CALCUTTA MADRAS KARACHI LAHORE DACCA
CAPE TOWN SALISBURY NAIROBI IBADAN ACCRA
KUALA LUMPUR HONG KONG

First edition 1959
Reprinted 1960, 1961 *and* 1963

Printed in Great Britain

CONTENTS

PREFACE

THE field covered by this book is much the same as that in my *Outline of Monetary Economics*, to which it can perhaps be regarded as an introduction. In addition, this book has the virtue of having been written more recently, so that this is the first treatment of English banking institutions, in book form, which is able to take full advantage of the developments of our understanding of the banking system which have occurred in the last few years.

I should like to express my thanks to Mr. Colin Mayhew for many useful criticisms of my first draft. I must also express my deep appreciation to Mr. Kurt Klappholz for his many detailed criticisms. Finally, my thanks go to Miss Stella Adamson for her patience and efficiency in typing the manuscript.

A. C. L. DAY

London
October, 1958.

Chapter One

MONEY, INCOME, AND WEALTH

THE economies of all the countries which are of any significance in the modern world are monetary economies. Whether they are capitalist or socialist, free enterprise or controlled, manufacturing or primary-producing, they all have the common characteristic that they make extensive use of money.

The most important use of money is in settling by far the larger part of transactions between different individuals or organizations in modern economies. It is true that some barter transactions still take place: I may exchange goods which I do not want for goods which I prefer, if I can find someone whose preferences lie the other way; or I may pay for services in kind, as by giving the gardener a meal instead of money. But such transactions are quite insignificant in modern economies, primarily because they are so difficult to organize in any economic system which is based on an extensive and complicated division of labour. If I want to get rid of my car in order to increase the size of my library, I shall find it very difficult and probably impossible to discover a person who has the books I should like and would prefer to own my car. Yet by selling the car for money and using the proceeds to buy books, the operation becomes easy. The man who buys my car may have received an inheritance in the form of stocks and shares which he has sold; the man who sells me the books may want the money to pay taxes; but since money can be used to settle any transaction, we are all easily satisfied, whereas without a medium of exchange, modern complex economies would be quite unworkable.

One implication of the fact that most transactions are settled in money is that most incomes are received in the form of money; this must obviously be so, since the receipt of an income is itself a transaction. If a workman receives £10 for a week's labour, the £10 are his income for that week, which arises out of a transaction involving the exchange of a week's labour services for £10. While all receipts of income involve a transaction, the reverse is by no means true. For example, if I lend £10 to a friend, neither of us has thereby received an income; our transaction has been purely financial. Again, transactions may produce incomes, but the total income produced may be much less than the total value of transactions which have taken place. If, for example, a miller buys £100 worth of wheat from a peasant farmer, buys the services of labour for £40, and sells the flour which is produced for £180, the total value of transactions which have taken place is £320 (100+40+180) but the total income produced is £180, which is the value of the final output which is produced (in the form of flour). Of this £180, an income of £100 accrues to the peasant farmer and £40 each to the workers as wages and to the miller as profits.

Since most processes of production pass through

several stages like this, it is clear that the total value of transactions in an economy in any given period is much greater than the income accruing in that period. Moreover, there will generally be many more stages than in our simplified case; for example, the farmer may in turn have bought seeds or labour or paid rent to someone else.

Money and Other Forms of Wealth

In addition to the close relationship between the study of money and the study of incomes, which arises from the fact that most incomes accrue in the form of money, there is an equally close relationship between the study of money and the study of wealth. A considerable part of the wealth of most transactors (a term which includes both individual households and organizations such as firms and the government) is held in the form of money. To a large extent, this also derives directly from the fact that most transactions are settled in money. This means that it is (generally speaking) advantageous to hold some money, in order to make payments which are due in the relatively near future and to be prepared for unpredictable contingencies.

While money is an important kind of wealth, it is by no means the only kind. It is useful to distinguish two main kinds of wealth, namely real wealth and claims. In present-day circumstances, money is in the latter category.

The basic difference between claims and real wealth arises from the fact that every claim is offset by a corresponding liability of some other transactor, so that if

we are adding up the total wealth of an economy, all
claims by one member of the economy against another
cancel out against the corresponding liabilities. The
only claims which are wealth from the viewpoint of
the economy as a whole, as opposed to that of individual
transactors, are claims against foreigners. Correspondingly, liabilities to foreigners must be offset against the
total wealth of the economy. Thus the economy's total
wealth consists of all its real wealth, plus any claims
against foreigners, minus any liabilities to them.

Real wealth consists of physical assests, such as
machines, houses and stocks of raw materials, goods in
process and finished products. These assets can be
used to produce other goods, or to produce useful
services, or can themselves be consumed at some future
time. Claims, on the other hand, reflect a legal obliga-
tion of some other transactor. The simplest kind of
claim is an IOU, which acknowledges a debt owed by
one person to another; the creditor has a claim against
the debtor to be paid the amount expressed in the
IOU. *Bills of exchange* are, in effect, dated IOUs; they
are a promise to pay a fixed sum of money on a given
date in the relatively near future; commonly they are
issued for three months. Documents of this kind,
with which we shall be extensively concerned in later
chapters, are often issued by governments, when they
are usually known as Treasury bills. Borrowing by
issuing bills is also quite often used as a means of
financing commercial operations, such as importing
and exporting; such bills are known as commercial
bills. The borrower who issues a bill pays for the

privilege of borrowing by paying interest on the sum he borrows. He does this by repaying a rather larger sum than he borrows: if he borrows £100 for three months, and the rate of interest payable on this kind of claim is 4 per cent. per annum, the promise will be made to pay £101 in three months' time.

Bonds are another important kind of claim; they are a method of borrowing for relatively long periods, of several years or more. This method of borrowing is used both by governments and by industrial and commercial firms; bonds issued by firms are commonly known as 'debentures'. A bond consists of a promise to pay a given sum of money annually for a given number of years (as interest) and to repay the capital sum borrowed at the end of the period. If the rate of interest currently payable on bonds is 5 per cent. a firm might borrow £100 for twenty years by issuing a promise to pay £5 per year for twenty years, and at the end of that time to repay the £100. Bonds may also be issued with no maturity date; in that case, no provision is made for repayment, and interest is payable indefinitely into the future. In general, only governments can borrow in this way; as an example, the British Government has in the past issued promises to pay £2. 10s. 0d. per annum for an indefinite period; these bonds are known as 2½ per cent. Consols.

A third kind of claim is the *equity share*. This does not promise any fixed income to its owner, but instead gives him a claim to a share in whatever profits are made by the firm which issues the share. Instead of owning a claim to a payment which is fixed in terms of money, the owner of an equity share is, literally, an owner of a share in the assets of the company. If the company is wound up, he has a claim to a share in the sale value of its assets, after all the company's creditors (including owners of its debentures) have been paid. Meanwhile, when the company is trading, the equity shareholder receives his share of whatever profits are earned and are distributed by the board of directors of the company. Obviously, the equity shareholder runs the risks that the firm will be operated unsuccessfully, so that there are no profits or even that it goes bankrupt, and that the directors may choose not to distribute all the profits that are earned. The latter risk is less serious than the former; if profits are made but not distributed, the assets held by the firm increase, and this usually increases its power to earn profits in the future, thus eventually (but perhaps very remotely) benefiting the shareholders. In order that they may protect themselves as well as they can against both of these risks, equity shareholders have the right to elect the directors of the company. In addition, the shareholder in a limited liability company knows that, even if the company goes bankrupt, his total loss is limited to the amount he has paid for the share.[1]

The bill, the bond, and equity share all possess the feature in common that they can easily be bought and sold on organized markets. The market for bonds and

[1] Plus any unpaid contributions to the share, if any; some shares are not 'fully paid-up', and their owners may be asked by the company to contribute the remaining sum; but the amount of these unpaid contributions is always certain and known to the shareholder.

shares is the stock exchange; the market for bills is frequently known as the money market or the discount market.[1] This market consists of the group of firms (operating in London in and around Lombard Street) which are willing to discount bills of exchange; this means that they will buy them before maturity for a price rather less than their face value; the amount of the face value is collected from the debtor on the maturity date. Stock exchanges are markets in a rather different sense; they do not consist of a group of firms, but places where bonds and shares are bought and sold; specialized firms carry out these transactions for their clients.

In addition to the bill, the bond, and the share, there are other kinds of claim which can be bought and sold on organized markets, but which will not be our concern in subsequent pages. An example is the preference share, whose characteristics lie between those of a debenture and an ordinary equity share; it gives a claim to any profits which a company earns, up to a maximum percentage; this claim has priority over the claims of the ordinary shareholders.

Finally, before considering the characteristics of money as a form of wealth, mention must be made of the many kinds of claim for which there is no organized market. Debts between individuals, trading debts between firms, debts of firms to individuals and the

---

[1] The former expression can be made to exaggerate the significance of the market; it is not money itself which is bought and sold, but claims to be paid a fixed sum of money in complete settlement of a debt at a time in the near future; the latter expression is therefore the more accurate.

reverse, claims of individuals against life insurance companies, and of hire purchase companies against individuals are among the many examples of such non-negotiable claims. Their importance should not be under-rated, even though we shall not be very much concerned with them, because our main preoccupation in considering claims will be with those for which organized markets exist.

Now that we have considered all these forms of claims, we can return to our discussion of money. Up to the earlier decades of this century, much money was in a form of real wealth, namely gold and silver. These conditions are now past, and need not detain us; today, all money used within advanced economies is merely a claim.

Money is a claim in two senses. In the first place, it is a debt owed to its owner by the government or a bank. This is to be seen most clearly in the case of a bank deposit. If I have a deposit at a bank, the bank is in debt to me, and records this in its accounts as a liability. Correspondingly, I have a claim against the bank, which I can exercise in various ways. I can give the bank instructions (normally by drawing a cheque) to transfer its debt to the credit of some other person; in this way, I can make a payment to that other person, in a very convenient manner. Alternatively, I can ask the bank to repay its debt to me, by withdrawing it; the bank settles by payment in some other form of money —in England this means by payment of Bank of England notes or of coin. The latter can be regarded as notes stamped on metal which are issued by the Royal

Mint, that is, by the Government; they are only used for small transactions.

Formally, Bank of England notes, like bank deposits, are a debt. On their face, they bear the words 'I Promise to pay the Bearer on Demand the sum of One Pound' (or whatever is the value of the note), signed by the Chief Cashier of the Bank of England. In fact, however, this promise is merely a relic of the days (before 1914) when the Bank of England would settle its debt in golden sovereigns. Today, the Bank of England note is legal tender for all sums, which means that a creditor must be willing to accept settlement duly made in Bank of England notes. Anyone who takes a pound note to the Bank of England and asks for a pound will merely be given another pound note.

Despite this slight absurdity, people continue to use Bank of England notes happily. The reason is that they are, like other kinds of money, a claim in a more significant sense than that implied by the legal formalities. Money can be defined as a claim which is generally acceptable in settlement of debts. Thus money can be used as a way of staking a claim over any good, service or other claim which is on the market. If I have money, I have access to everything else which is purchasable. If I own sufficient coin, bank deposits or bank notes, I can lay claim to anything which is on the market, quite directly, without any further intermediary. This feature distinguishes money from all other forms of wealth.

Two Decisions for Transactors

The study of the decisions of transactors about their

B

holdings of wealth will be of central importance in the argument of the rest of this book. As an introduction to the chapters which follow it is, therefore, helpful to summarize what these decisions are. For our purpose, there are two major decisions, which it will be convenient to keep rather distinct from one another, even though they are very closely related.

The first kind consists of the plans made by each transactor to alter the total amount of wealth he possesses. We can reasonably assume that each transactor regularly makes plans (say at the beginning of each week) about the changes he wishes to make during the week in the total amount of wealth he possesses. Typical of these decisions is a plan by a householder not to spend the whole of the income he receives during the week on current consumption (such as food, travel, and rent), but to put some of it by in order to increase his total wealth. Another decision of this kind is a plan by a firm to hold more real wealth (such as factories or machines).[1]

The second kind of decision is concerned not with additions to wealth but with the form in which existing wealth shall be held. For example, a private individual may decide to switch the wealth he has accumulated or inherited in the past from one kind of share to another, or from bonds into shares, or into money. Similar plans may be made by other transactors who hold wealth. Of the same general character and of the same kind of significance are plans made by debtors to switch from

[1] Strictly speaking, this real wealth is the property of the firm's shareholders.

owing one kind of debt to another: as we have seen, debts are in effect negative wealth. As an example, the government may choose to switch from owing debt by issuing bills and issue more bonds instead.

Obviously, the distinction that has been drawn in the previous two paragraphs between decisions about changes in total wealth and decisions about the form in which wealth shall be held cannot be pushed too far. In particular, any decision to add to total wealth must necessarily also involve a decision about the form in which that additional wealth is held.

That there is a close relationship between the two decisions can be shown by considering for a moment why transactors choose to hold wealth. Broadly speaking, they do so because it gives them some kind of return—some sort of yield or income. I hold money or own a car, largely because these forms of wealth give me a yield of convenience. I own bonds because they give me an income, in the form of the interest they earn. Different kinds of wealth which yield an income may do so in different ways; it may be as interest (as with a bond) or as profits (as with a share). Again, the income may accrue because of the ability of some forms of real wealth (e.g. machines) to help produce a saleable output. Or again, the income may arise because the selling price of an asset (such as a picture) increases over time, so that someone who holds it can sell it for more than he paid for it.

In all these cases, the precise character and value of the yield of convenience or income which is provided by the ownership of wealth depends on the kind of wealth that is owned. Since the decision to own wealth is usually determined by these prospective yields, it is clear that a transactor will, in the final analysis, be influenced by the same forces in making both kinds of decision. In other words, it is impossible to distinguish between the two kinds of transaction, in so far as transactors' *motivations* are concerned. The motivations lying behind both decisions to add to wealth and decisions to change the form in which wealth is held are the desire of the rational economic man to make the best of the circumstances in which he finds himself.

In spite of this, the distinction that has been drawn is a valid one, in terms of the *consequences* of the two kinds of transaction. The main reason for this is that the total amount of wealth in existence at any time is very much larger than any single week's addition to that stock of wealth. This means that decisions about the form in which additions to wealth shall be held are quantitatively relatively insignificant in relation to decisions about the forms in which old wealth shall be held. This means that we can avoid detailed investigation of the question of the forms in which additions to wealth are held, and concentrate on the two questions of the size of total additions to wealth and of the forms in which old wealth is held.

The significance of the distinction between the two kinds of decision is that each kind is particularly closely related to one of the two main problems with which we shall be concerned. Decisions about additions to wealth are particularly closely related to the theory of the determination of the level of income, which will be our concern in Chapters 2–5. Decisions about the form in which wealth shall be held are particularly closely related to the theory of interest rates and the operation of the banking system, which will be our concern in Chapters 6–9.

While we shall make extensive use of this distinction between the theories of income determination and of interest rate determination, it must be emphasized that this distinction is only a first approximation to reality. In practice, changes in interest rates have effects on the level of income and changes in the level of income affect interest rates. In isolating the two, we are simply taking a first step, which has the virtue that it involves the biggest movement towards reality which is consistent with a simple theory.

Chapter Two

INCOME

An individual's income consists of what he receives in a period of time as a result of the ownership of property or of his active contribution to the productive process. Examples of the latter kind of income are wages and salaries. Examples of earnings from property are the interest earned by bond-holders, the profits earned by shareholders and the rent earned by landlords. As we saw in the previous chapter, these receipts usually accrue in the form of money, but they may possibly accrue in other ways.

It should be noted that statements about income refer to a period of time. Income is, in fact, a flow, and we can only measure a flow by considering it in relation to a stated time period. We shall mainly be concerned with incomes per week and incomes per year.

If we try to give a perfectly satisfactory definition of income we run into awkward problems. Fortunately we can for the most part ignore them, but it is necessary to indicate the kinds of difficulty that arise. In each case, we shall find it necessary to draw arbitrary boundaries between those receipts which are regarded as income and those which are not. It will be convenient if the boundaries we adopt are the same as those which have been used in the United Kingdom by the income tax authorities; they can easily be used as the basis of our estimates of the income of the country as a whole.

One difficulty that arises in defining precise boundaries concerns goods which are both produced and consumed by the same person or family. Logically, it is not very satisfactory to say that if a farmer rears a pig and kills it for consumption within the family, the operation does not give rise to any income, whereas if he kills it, sells it for money and buys beef with the proceeds his income is increased by the price for which he sold the pig. Nevertheless, convenience often drives us into this rather illogical situation; at least no one attempts to regard the cabbages I produce in my back garden as part of my income. Yet the illogicality of any arbitrary boundary must be conceded: to exclude everything both produced and consumed within the household would imply that a subsistence farmer has no income.

Closely analogous is the difficulty arising from the need to decide whether the services provided by certain kinds of property (such as a house, a car or a piano) are to be regarded as income. In terms of pure logic, it is hard to distinguish between the receipts in the form of convenience that I enjoy from occupying a house which I own from those I enjoy from running my car. Nevertheless, the former are regarded as income by the income tax authorities while the latter are not; once again, an arbitrary line has to be drawn somewhere.

A second difficulty arises from doubts as to whether or not to count capital gains as income. Here, again, an arbitrary convention is necessary. If I buy a car or a share and sell it again at a profit, the gain is not regarded as an income. On the other hand, if the whole nature of the business I am running is based on such profits (as a car dealer who buys cars to sell them again), the gains are regarded as an income.

Nothing further need be said about these arbitrary boundaries to the flows we define as income; but once they are drawn, they must be adhered to rigorously.

Output and Income

We must now look into the relationship between the total output of a country and the total income of all the people in that country. In doing so, it will be convenient to avoid the complications that arise from foreign trade, by assuming that our country has no economic relationships with outsiders: that it is a 'closed economy'. This assumption will be maintained in the next few chapters. It will also simplify matters if we assume that there is no government; this assumption will be dropped later in Chapter 3.

In adding up the total national output, it is important not to count the same thing more than once. If in a given year a farmer grows wheat and the wheat is milled into flour, then the value of the year's output is the value of the flour. It is not the value of the wheat plus the value of the flour; the wheat has been incorporated into the flour. Similarly, if last year's harvest of wheat is milled into flour this year, the total output of this year is simply the difference between the value of the wheat and the value of the flour. The value of the wheat itself has already been counted as part of last year's output, and it would be double-counting to include it again; the value of the output produced this year is equal to the total value of the output, less the value of the raw materials used up in the process of production (in this case, the wheat).

Again in the statistical work of adding up the total national output, for the sake of comparing it with the total national income, we must make sure that we include in 'output' all those goods and services whose production leads to the receipt of income, and that we avoid including any other goods and services. Thus, neither the cabbages I grow in my back garden nor the services given by my car should be included in the national output, whereas the services provided by my house are included.

If we define output and income consistently, by following the same rules in defining each of them, then the total national income in any period must necessarily be the same as the total value of the national output. This is a most important identity, which applies to any closed economy. In commonsense terms, output results from the use of productive services; income is acquired from the provision of productive services. In any period, the value of productive services used must be equal to the value of productive services provided.

This can be seen by extending the numerical example given in the previous chapter. There, we imagined a simple case where the total output consisted of £180 worth of flour, and where a farmer received an income of £100 and a worker and a miller each received £40; their total income is £180. If our economy consisted of 100 people of each of these three kinds, each just like his neighbour, the total income of the economy would be £18,000, which is just equal to the output of flour produced.

In reality, the problem of working out the national income is much more complicated than this, because many different kinds of commodity are in fact produced. Nevertheless, the principles involved are just the same. The national accounts of our simple economy could be represented as follows:

Income	£	*Output*	£
Farmers' Income	10,000	Value of flour pro-	
Millers' Income	4,000	duced	18,000
Workers' Income	4,000		
	18,000		18,000

More generally, we can represent the national accounts of any economy in something like the following form:

Income	£000	*Output*	£000
Wages	10,000	Value of output of	
Salaries	2,000	currently pro-	
Profits	8,000	duced goods and	
Other incomes	2,000	services	22,000
	22,000		22,000

Two modifications of this simple kind of statement will be useful for our purposes: both of them arise out of the item entitled 'profits'. The first is that some profits may not be distributed to shareholders, but instead are retained by the company and are added to the total wealth held by the company. These 'undistributed profits' are a form of income for the shareholders, because they are ultimately the property of the shareholders, who own the assets of the company. Nevertheless, income accruing in the form of undistributed profits is significantly different from income accruing as distributed profits; it is not possible for the shareholders to use the former directly for purchasing goods and services, whereas they can obviously spend the latter as they wish.

The other modification arises from the fact that most forms of real wealth deteriorate with time or with use. A manufacturing firm, in calculating its total costs of production, must take account of the depreciation of its machinery and buildings. It must make provision for maintaining the value of its real wealth, either by current maintenance or by provision for eventual replacement, and usually both. If it fails to do so, the day will come when it has no machines to keep production going. Similarly, holders of other capital assets which provide an income must make provision for depreciation; on the definitions of income we are following,[1] the only case of this which affects transactors other than firms is the need for householders to make provision for house maintenance.

In the national accounts set out above, no mention was made of these needs to cover depreciation; we

[1] The only capital equipment owned by householders consists of houses; they therefore have no other real capital to maintain on the definitions normally used in national income accounting.

added up the whole of national output, and in that total some part would in fact have to be earmarked for depreciation. We can construct an alternative set of accounts which represent income and output net of these depreciation provisions; instead of representing 'gross' national income as we did earlier, we can now represent 'net' national income. If we suppose that £2 million worth of output has to be used each year to cover depreciation of the country's real wealth, all of which, we have assumed,[1] is held by firms, then our national accounts, reckoned net, look like this:

Net National Income	£000	Net National Output	£000
Wages	10,000	Value of net output	
Salaries	2,000	of goods and	
Net profits (after depreciation provisions)	6,000	services	20,000
Other incomes	2,000		
	20,000		20,000

Both the gross and the net measures of national income and output are commonly used in economic analysis. It is a rather easier statistical task to measure gross national income than net, because there are many snags in deciding what is the appropriate allowance to make for depreciation of fixed capital;[2] and in fact any method is to some extent arbitrary.

[1] With the exception of houses.
[2] Changes in stocks of materials, goods in process, and finished output are allowed for before arriving at the gross figure—as we did in our example of the miller and the farmer.

Saving and Investment

As a preliminary to a discussion of the theory of the determination of the level of national income, which will be our concern in the next two chapters, it will now be convenient to present the national accounts in a more detailed manner, which will prove relevant to our later theoretical discussion. On the one hand, we can ask what the recipients of income will do with their income; on the other hand, we can ask something about the constituents of the national output.

We can say that receivers of income will either spend it on current consumption, or put it aside in some form or other and so add to their total holdings of wealth. In the former case, we say they 'consume' and in the latter case they 'save'. In an economy where there is no government and therefore no taxes, the whole of income must, by definition, be used in one or other of these ways.

Once again, we have to make a rather arbitrary division between consumption and saving. It is obvious that if I use this year's income to buy food, travel or entertainment, I am consuming; it is equally clear that if I buy a bond or a share with it I am adding to my wealth and saving. The awkward items are the so-called consumer durable goods, such as cars, pianos, and clothing. Strictly speaking, if I buy a piano with this year's income, I am adding to my wealth; nevertheless, it is usual not to count such expenditure as saving, but as consumption. To do so is not really very satisfactory, but it is the usual procedure; the only important purchases of real wealth by individuals which are generally regarded as saving are purchases of houses. Thus, the boundary at least has the convenience of being the same as the one used earlier to distinguish wealth which is regarded as giving rise to income from wealth which is not so regarded.

It follows from all this that the greater part of saving by individuals must take the form of additional holdings of claims. Thus, I may put my savings into bonds, shares, bills or money; I also save if I use my income to buy a house; but any other form of expenditure by a private individual on real wealth is regarded as consumption.

We can now turn to the output side of the accounts, and look at what happens to the total output that is produced in our country in a given period of time. One alternative is obvious from the preceding discussion: a part of the national output is used for current consumption by households. All their purchases of food and entertainment, of cars and pianos, are uses of output which we have classified as consumption. The whole of the rest of the national output, which is not consumed, is added to the country's holding of real wealth. This process is known as 'investment'.[1] It takes

---

[1] Investment in this sense *must* be distinguished from the popular use of the word. In the popular use, 'investment' simply means the acquisition of an income-yielding asset by an individual or firm. In the economists' sense it refers exclusively to those acquisitions of income-yielding assets which are also additions to the *community's* holding of real wealth. Thus, the purchase of a bond, an equity share or a *second-hand* house is *not* investment in our sense, whereas the purchase of a new house or machine is. This distinction is most important for the understanding of the whole of modern economic theory.

two main forms: fixed investment and investment in stocks. The former includes additions to real wealth held in such forms as machines, factories, and houses; the latter includes additions to stocks of raw materials, of goods in the process of production and of finished products awaiting sale.

Just like income and output as a whole, both investment and saving can be measured either before or after making allowance for depreciation of fixed capital. Gross investment consists of total additions to real wealth, including that part which replaces old equipment and buildings that have worn out; net investment excludes this replacement element. Similarly, gross saving includes the sums set aside to pay for replacement of fixed assets as they wear out, while net saving does not.

It may be noted that it is quite possible for net investment (and saving) to be negative, if total additions to real wealth in a given period are inadequate to replace all the equipment and buildings that are wearing out (or if depreciation provisions are inadequate to finance replacement). Again, it is quite possible for there to be negative investment in stocks; this happens if total stocks are reduced. The word disinvestment is used to describe negative investment of these kinds.

We now have two concepts, saving and investment, which are of basic importance in the analysis of the forces determining national income. Saving consists of that part of income which is not consumed; investment consists of that part of output which is added to the country's holding of real wealth.

There are two important things we can say about the ways in which we have defined the two words 'savings' and 'investment'. In the first place, decisions about whether or not to save are usually (though by no means always) made by transactors other than those who make decisions about investment. Secondly, it follows inevitably from the way we have defined the words, that saving and investment are always inevitably equal, if we look at the accounts for any past period.

The fact that decisions to save are commonly made independently of decisions to invest lies at the heart of the theory of income determination. Generally speaking, decisions not to consume current income are made by households, who are the final recipients of income. But there also are two very important cases where a decision to save is commonly made by firms. Some reference has already been made to these cases. The first arises where we are measuring investment and saving gross—i.e. including allowance for depreciation of fixed assets. A prudent firm sets aside financial provision (gross saving) for the replacement (gross investment) of buildings and equipment as they wear out. The second case arises even where we are measuring saving and investment net of depreciation provisions. If a firm decides not to distribute the whole of the profits it earns, then the decision is made by the board of directors of the firm on behalf of the shareholders that a part of their income shall be put aside and added to their total wealth. In several post-war years in Britain, firms have chosen to save such a large part of their profits, and households have chosen to save such a small part of their incomes, that business saving has been quantitatively more important than household saving.

While decisions to save are commonly made by households, decisions to invest are nearly always made by firms. For example, a decision to install a new machine is a decision of a kind which is always made by firms. The only decision to add to real wealth that is commonly made by households is the decision to buy a house; all other purchases by households of durable consumer goods have been counted as consumption and not as additions to real wealth.

The second feature of savings and investment in the set of accounts for any past period is that they are necessarily equal. Why this should be so can easily be seen, in either of two ways. One way is to look at what happens to the income and the output; the other is to look at the additions that have been made to wealth in the hands of various kinds of transactor.

As we have seen, in our simplified economy (in which there is neither government nor foreign trade) there are only two ways in which income can be used and there are only two ways in which output can be used. Income can either be consumed or saved; together, these two possibilities cover the whole of the national income. As for output, there are again by definition only two possibilities: it can either be consumed, or it goes into additional holdings of real wealth: in which case we say that it is invested. We have already seen that the national income for any

c

period is necessarily equal to the national output in the same period. From this it follows quite simply that saving and investment are necessarily equal in the national accounts. The proof of this identity (which applies whether all the concepts are measured gross or net of depreciation provisions) can conveniently be summed up in the following way:

National Income ≡ (is numerically identical with) Consumption *plus* Saving

National Output ≡ Consumption *plus* Investment

But National Income ≡ National Output

Therefore Investment ≡ Saving

The other way in which we can understand this necessary identity between saving and investment in the national accounts is to look at the additions that have been made to the wealth owned by the various transactors in our economy. The commonsense point here is simply that the additional real wealth in the economy (i.e. the investment that has taken place) must be owned by somebody. In most cases, the owner will be a firm; we can concentrate on this case by assuming that households neither acquire nor sell houses; this simplifies the analysis. A firm which acquires additional real wealth may have paid for the new investment in one of four ways. Firstly, it may fail to distribute the whole of its profits to its shareholders. Secondly, it may have borrowed from households, as by issuing new bonds or shares. Thirdly, it may have borrowed from banks and other financial institutions. Fourthly, it may have run down its holdings of claims; for example, it may reduce its holdings of cash, or it may sell other claims it owns, as by selling bonds and using the proceeds to pay for the new machine. Firms in the country as a whole may use any or all of these methods of financing investment; whichever is followed, there must be corresponding saving by income recipients, taken as a whole. If the first method of finance is used, firms are choosing to save on behalf of their shareholders. In all the other three cases firms have passed on claims of some sort or other to other transactors, and so other transactors taken as a group must be holding that additional total quantity of claims. These net additional claims must be held by transactors who are adding to their total holdings of claims—i.e. who are saving. This is obvious if the claims go straight to these transactors, as will commonly be the case in the second and fourth examples above. In the case where firms borrow from financial institutions such as banks, so giving claims to those institutions, the same thing happens at one remove. As we shall see in more detail in Chapters 6 and 7, the distinguishing characteristic of the business of these institutions is that they are intermediaries between transactors who wish to issue one kind of claim and other transactors who wish to hold a different kind of claim.

Thus, whatever may be the way in which firms finance investment, somewhere there must be corresponding additional holdings of claims (saving) by some income recipients. We have therefore arrived at the same conclusion as before: in the national accounts saving and investment are necessarily the same. The argument has been rather more cumbersome than that in the first demonstration given; either demonstration can be employed, and they both have their uses. The first has the virtue of simplicity; the second has the advantage of showing what are the implications of the savings-investment analysis in the markets for claims.

Chapter Three

THE LEVELS OF INCOME, ACTIVITY, AND OUTPUT

THE explanation of the determination of the level of national income follows quite directly from two things that have been pointed out in the previous chapter. One is that we have defined the words 'saving' and 'investment' in such a way that the two are inevitably identical in the national income accounts for any past period. The other is that plans to save and plans to invest are commonly made by different transactors, acting independently of each other.

Since plans about saving and investment are often made independently, there is no reason to suppose that total plans to save in any week or year will be equal to total plans to invest in the same period. For example, firms may choose to increase or decrease their investment plans for next year to levels higher or lower than this year's. Such a decision is made quite independently of the plans of households to save, so there is no reason at all why the change in the investment plans of firms should be accompanied by a corresponding change in households' plans to save.

In spite of this, it remains true that *realized* saving and *realized* investment must be equal. The reconciliation between this necessary equality and the possible inequality between investment and savings *plans* is not hard to find. What happens is that some transactors find that the plans they had made for the period cannot, in the event, be precisely carried out.

This discrepancy between realized events and transactors' plans can come about in different ways. The most important arises from the fact that most firms are unaware of changes in the plans made by other firms. Thus, if a considerable number of manufacturing firms decide to invest less than they did in the last period (by building fewer new factories and installing fewer machines), the effect is to reduce the incomes of the people in the building and machinery industries. In turn, these people buy less goods of all kinds. There is, however, no reason to suppose that shopkeepers will be aware that this is going to happen; they will probably have planned their purchases from wholesalers on the assumption that their sales would be at the same level as in the preceding period. If so, shopkeepers will come to find that the stocks of goods left on their shelves are larger than they had planned. We can describe this by saying that the shopkeepers find they have made 'unplanned investment'; they hold more real wealth (in the form of stocks of unsold goods) than they had intended to hold.[1]

It is possible to develop this theme at length, but the important point is indicated by this example. For the period under consideration, investment plans were

[1] Similarly, if spending and incomes rise because some firms decide to install more machinery, a likely result will be that shopkeepers will make unexpectedly large sales so that their stocks fall unexpectedly; they make 'unplanned disinvestment'.

reduced, but in the event realized investment in the economy as a whole did not fall as much as had been planned, because of the unplanned investment in stocks by shopkeepers.

This reconciliation of the discrepancy between investment and saving plans is crucial in the explanation of the determination of the level of national income. As we have just seen, the plans of some (or all) transactors are not precisely realized. But, if a transactor's plans are not precisely realized, it can be expected that he will change his plans for subsequent periods. Our example of the shopkeepers indicates clearly the kind of thing that will happen. The shopkeepers find themselves with unexpectedly large stocks of goods on their shelves; it is likely that their reaction will be to reduce their orders from the manufacturers to levels below those of the preceding period, in order to reduce their stocks to reasonable levels again. We can say that the shopkeepers plan to 'disinvest', by reducing their holdings of real wealth.

In turn, this action by the shopkeepers upsets the plans of the manufacturers, who find they have more finished goods in their warehouses than they had intended. It is reasonable to assume that the manufacturers react by reducing their output, which in turn reduces the incomes of households, and consequently their expenditure.

Thus we have a cumulative decline in the level of national income as a consequence of the initial reduction in investment plans of firms. The important question that remains is, where does this decline stop? Similarly, we should ask where the expansion of the level of income would stop, if there had been an initial expansionary force such as an increase in the level of investment planned by firms.

The answer to these questions depends on the fact that the level of income can only be in equilibrium (that is, have no tendency to change over time) if total savings plans are equal to total investment plans. Only if there is this consistency of plans can it be possible for the plans of all transactors to be precisely realized; only if each transactor's plans are precisely realized will transactors leave their plans unchanged in the next period; and only if plans are unchanged from one period to the next will there be no tendency for the level of income to alter.

How, then, does it ever come about the total savings plans are equal to total investment plans? The answer is simply that, as the level of income changes, plans to save also change. A household that saves £1 out of a weekly income of £10 might save nothing out of a weekly income of £7, whereas it might save £3 out of a weekly income of £16. In our example, the decline in national income following the reduction in households' plans for investment by firms would lead to a reduction in plans to save. Sooner or later, this process would have gone so far that incomes were so small that savings plans had fallen to an extent as great as the original fall in firms' investment plans. At this level, and only at this level, is it possible for a new equilibrium in the level of national income to be established.

The Multiplier

If we make two quite plausible assumptions, it is

possible to calculate very easily what will be the change in the equilibrium level of income which arises as a result of a change in the level of investment plans.[1] The first assumption, which is broadly borne out by the available statistical information, is that there is a simple and stable relationship between changes in the level of national income and changes in the level of saving. The 'marginal propensity to save' describes this relationship; it is defined as the ratio of a change in the level of plans to save to the associated change in the level of income. To take the example just given; a rise in a household's income by £3 a week from £7 to £10 leads to a rise in its saving by £1 per week; a rise by £6, from £10 to £16, leads to a rise in saving by £2; and vice versa for a fall. Thus, in this case and within these ranges of income, this household's marginal propensity to save is $\frac{1}{3}$. If the whole community is made up of similar households, and all saving is done by households, then the marginal propensity to save of the country as a whole is also $\frac{1}{3}$.

The second assumption is that no price changes are occurring. There are many plausible circumstances in which this assumption is realistic; at the same time, its limitations must be recognized. The experience of most manufacturing countries in the greater part of the twentieth century has been that the price level of manufactured output as a whole does not vary very much when there is an appreciable amount of

[1] The reader should be warned that such calculations, while simple within the confines of our 'model', are by no means simple in practice.

unemployment of men and machines. In such circumstances, historical experience suggests that the main consequence of a change in the level of demand for manufactured goods is a change in the level of output and of activity—the level of prices remaining more or less unchanged.

When income rises and prices remain constant, the people who are receiving the incomes can buy a bigger volume of goods and services. Such a rise is known as a rise in real incomes—members of the community, taken as a whole, have available more goods and services. On the other hand, if prices and incomes both alter by the same percentage, there has been a change in money income, but real incomes have remained unchanged. If my money income doubles but the prices of all the things I buy also double, my income will buy me just the same volume of goods as before—my real income is unchanged.

There are two sets of circumstance in which we cannot assume that changes in demand do not lead to appreciable price changes. Both of these exceptions are very important, and will be discussed in Chapter 4. One is the case of countries producing agricultural and other primary products—in the absence of State intervention, prices of these goods usually alter substantially when the demand for them alters. The other case is that of a fully-employed manufacturing economy: a rise in demand for the output of such an economy cannot be satisfied by increasing the level of activity, because men and machines are already fully employed. Given sufficient time, it can be satisfied by increasing the level of output produced by a given labour force—in other words, by increasing productivity. But there is a limit to the speed with which this can happen, and for the rest, the most likely consequence of a rise in demand in these conditions is a rise in prices.

The relationship between the change in the level of investment and the consequential change in the level of income, output, and activity is very simple when no price changes are taking place. In the new equilibrium situation, it is necessary for the level of savings plans to be equal to the new level of investment plans: in other words, savings plans must change by an amount equal to the change in investment plans. Since savings plans vary with the level of income (to an extent measured by the value of the marginal propensity to save), there will be some new level of income at which savings plans will have changed sufficiently to satisfy our equilibrium condition.

If, for example, the only possible equilibrium is one involving an increase of £10 million in the level of savings plans, because the level of investment plans has risen by £10 million, and if the marginal propensity to save is $\frac{1}{3}$, then an increase in income of £30 million will call forth the required additional savings. The equilibrium increase in the level of income (i.e. an increase which restores consistency between investment and savings plans) is one of £30 million. This is three times the increase in investment plans we assumed. This ratio between the increase in the level of investment plans and the increase in the level of income in the new equilibrium is known as the 'multiplier'.

In this example, the value of the multiplier is three.[1]

The sole determinant of the size of this multiplier is (in the simple conditions we are assuming) the size of the marginal propensity to save. If this had been $\frac{1}{2}$, then an increase of income by only £20 million would have been sufficient to evoke the £10 million additional savings which are necessary for equilibrium. In this case, therefore, the multiplier would only be two.

The two numerical examples given illustrate the general rule; this is, that the multiplier is equal to the inverse of the marginal propensity to save (that is, to one divided by the marginal propensity to save; $1 \div \frac{1}{2} = 2$; $1 \div \frac{1}{3} = 3$). The equilibrium change in the level of income arising from a given change in investment expenditure is the larger the smaller is the marginal propensity to save, and vice versa.

The common sense of this result is quite simple. The initiating increase in the level of investment involves an equal increase in the level of income of the same magnitude for the people producing the goods and services which are now being bought by the firms who are investing more. These people in turn spend part of their additional incomes (saving the rest), and so create additional incomes for still more people. These people in turn spend part of their additional incomes (and again save the rest), so creating additional incomes for yet more people, and so on. Now it is reasonably obvious that the total increase in the level of national

[1] It should be emphasized that the new higher level of income will be maintained only if the increase in investment plans is permanent. A temporary increase in investment only raises income temporarily.

income will be the larger, the smaller are the leakages into saving at each round. If all the increase in income at the first round went to saving, there would be no additional incomes at the second round. If none of the additional incomes went to saving, then the level of income would keep expanding without limit. If (as is normal) part of additional income is saved and part spent, then the successive increases in the level of income get smaller and smaller, because each is only a fraction of the preceding one. Thus, if the addition to the level of investment is £10 million, and the marginal propensity to save is $\frac{1}{2}$, the first-round recipients of the corresponding £10 million of additional income would spend £5 million of it. This raises incomes by a further £5 million, of which a half is in turn spent (and a half saved). The level of income rises by another £2$\frac{1}{2}$ million. At the next round, the rise in expenditure and income is £1$\frac{1}{4}$ million. Thus, the level of income rises by steadily diminishing steps. Moreover, the level approaches a total increase of £20 million (10 + 5 + 2$\frac{1}{2}$ + 1$\frac{1}{4}$ + $\frac{5}{8}$ . . .). Theoretically, this increase takes an infinite time to work out, but in practice the level of income approaches very nearly to the equilibrium in a fairly small number of rounds. How long this means in terms of calendar time depends largely upon the time lags of firms and individuals in their responses to the changes in circumstances which have led to their plans not being precisely realized. It is probably reasonable to regard a period of one to three years as the interval which would usually elapse before practically full adjustment could be made towards a new equilibrium.

In practice, of course, new disturbances usually come along before full adjustment has been made to any given change in circumstances; analysis of real events is made so much more difficult.

The Government

Up to this point, we have been making two drastic simplifications in considering the working of our economy; we have assumed that there is no government and no foreign trade. The time has now come to relax the first of these limiting assumptions, and consider what happens when there is a government.

There are three main reasons why we have to pay particular attention to the role of the government. The first is that governments can impose taxes; the second is that they usually finance any kind of expenditure they like by borrowing; the third is that they are usually deeply concerned with the problems of stabilizing the economy. We shall be concerned with the last of these three points in our discussion of stabilization policy in Chapter 5; the other two will be our immediate concern.

Taxes can usefully be classified into three categories: taxes on income, taxes on expenditure, and taxes on capital. The British income and surtaxes are examples of the first group; the purchase tax and the excise duties on tobacco are examples of the second; death duties are an example of the third. We can ignore this third group for the purposes of this chapter; the effects on the level of income of changes in such capital taxes as exist in the United Kingdom are remote and probably quite slight.

Taxes on expenditure and on income are, on the other hand, very important. In their detailed economic effects they differ substantially; for example, the replacement of a tax on income by a tax on expenditure giving the same yield might have substantial influence on individuals' decisions to work and to spend. Nevertheless, they are sufficiently similar for us to neglect the differences between them. They both reduce the real incomes of the taxpayers to levels below those they would otherwise enjoy. This is obvious in the case of an income tax. A little reflection shows it is also true for taxes like the purchase tax: I have to pay more for many of the things I buy, and so my money income will buy less. Since the two kinds of tax can, to this extent, be regarded as being similar, it will greatly simplify matters if we assume that the only kind of tax in existence is an income tax. Moreover, it will be convenient to assume that everyone pays the same rate of income tax.

The second characteristic of governments which leads us to pay special attention to them is that they can usually finance any kind of expenditure they like by borrowing. Firms and private individuals can only borrow easily when they have some kind of asset available to act as security for the loan. Thus firms can usually borrow to build factories and most individuals can borrow to help buy a house because the factory or house can be taken over by the creditor in the event of default; again, firms can borrow for relatively short periods of time to finance holdings of stocks of goods. But it is difficult for firms or households to borrow when no concrete security can be given. Governments, on the other hand, can usually borrow solely on the basis of their own name, even though it is known that the goods which are to be bought with the borrowed money will be consumed immediately. Generally speaking, governments have little difficulty in borrowing even for purposes as destructive as fighting a war. Ultimately, this power of governments to borrow for any purpose is closely related to their power of taxation; anyone who lends to a government knows that it can raise the interest it owes to the lender by imposing taxes.

It is because of these two features of the government (that it can tax and that it can finance any kind of expenditure by borrowing) that we must pay separate attention to the role of the government in formulating the multiplier theory. In making this elaboration, it is convenient to ask two different questions. In the first place, we can ask what happens to the multiplier relationship, when the government is following a given set of policies about taxation and expenditure. In the second place, we can ask what will be the consequences of a change in the government's taxation or expenditure policies (or, of course, of a simultaneous change in both taxation and expenditure policies).

In asking the first question, we assume that the government has fixed the rate of taxation: income tax is so many shillings in the pound, whatever else may change. We also assume that the government has made decisions about expenditure policy. For example, it may have decided to spend a given sum of money, whatever may happen to tax revenues. Or it may have decided to spend a given proportion of tax revenues. Or again, it may be committed to policies which involve more expenditure when the level of income and activity in the country is low; for example, it may be committed to paying unemployment benefits.

Whatever may be the government's tax and expenditure policies, the effect of the introduction of the government on to the scene is, in principle, quite simple. By imposing taxes, the government reduces the spendable incomes of households. As a result, households both consume and save less than they otherwise would. How much less of each they will do can be measured by the marginal propensities to save and to consume. If the government takes away £3 a week of my income, and my marginal propensity to save out of the spendable income I receive is one-third, then my savings are reduced by £1. Similarly, my consumption will be reduced by £2, since my marginal propensity to consume out of spendable income is two-thirds. (All my spendable, post-tax, income must, by definition, go either to consumption or saving.)

It is quite conceivable that the government will use just the same proportion of the taxes it takes from me to buy currently produced goods and services as I would have spent on such goods and services in the absence of the taxes. In that case, the size of the multiplier is completely unaffected by the existence of the government. For example, if an equilibrium situation is disturbed by a rise in the level of investment by firms, what will be the rise in the level of income that will have occurred when equilibrium has been re-established? The answer is that it will be just the same as in the

D

absence of government action, because in effect the government is itself using a part of the additions to income received by each household in the same way as the households would have done.[1] If the government takes away half of every £1 of the extra income I received, of which I would have spent 13s. 4d. on currently produced goods and services, I now only spend 6s. 8d. out of the 10s. I have left. But in addition, we are assuming the government spends 6s. 8d. of the 10s. it receives in taxes on buying currently-produced goods and services; in aggregate, the increase in spending by myself and the government taken together is 13s. 4d., just as if I had had all the income to spend myself. The plans of all transactors (households, firms, and the government) are therefore consistent at the same level of income as they would be in the absence of the government.

If the government spends the whole of the additional tax receipts for buying currently-produced goods and services, the rise in the equilibrium level of income is larger: the multiplier is bigger than when the government is absent. In this case, the total additional purchases of goods and services out of each additional £1 of income received by a household is larger than in the absence of the government. If I receive an additional £1 and am left with it all, I may consume 13s. 4d. worth of additional goods, which leads to additional incomes of 13s. 4d. for the people who sold me those goods. If,

[1] Of course, the government may well use the money to buy different things from those the households would have bought. This means that different people benefit from the expansion of incomes; but *in aggregate* the effect is the same.

on the other hand, the government takes 10s. of my £1 as income tax, and spends it all, leaving me with 10s. of which I again spend two-thirds (6s. 8d.), then there are additional expenditures and incomes of 16s. 8d.

At the other extreme is the possibility that the government may actually spend less when incomes rise; for example, it may have to pay out less in unemployment benefits. Then, the multiplier will be much smaller than in the absence of government activities. It might be that government expenditure falls by 5s. for every £1 rise in national income; when national income rises, the government can save more (a bigger budget surplus) or needs to borrow less (a smaller budget deficit). At the same time, the government may take 10s. out of each additional £1 of income, as taxes, leaving 10s. over to households, of which we can again assume 6s. 8d. is consumed and the rest saved. Then the total additional expenditure on goods and services arising from £1 additional national income is only 1s. 8d.; household expenditure rises by 6s. 8d. but government expenditure falls by 5s. In such circumstances, the multiplier is very small; only a very small part of a rise of incomes is passed on to create further rises of incomes.

All these results can be summed up in an extension of our familiar principle, that in equilibrium planned saving must equal planned investment. The extension that is required is the inclusion of taxes and government expenditure. In the first place, we now find that national income can be used to pay taxes; we see that

National Income $\equiv$ Consumption *plus* Saving *plus* Taxes

In the second place, national output can also be used by the government in its purchases of currently produced goods and services; we see that

National Output $\equiv$ Consumption *plus* Investment *plus* Government Expenditure on current output

But since National Income and National Output are necessarily the same in size, and since Consumption enters into both of the identities just set out, we find that

Saving *plus* Taxes $\equiv$ Investment *plus* Government Expenditure

If we call the excess of Government Expenditure over Taxes Paid the 'Budget Deficit', it follows that

Saving $\equiv$ Investment $+$ Budget Deficit

This condition necessarily applies for past events, and it must apply for plans if they are to prove consistent.

The same solution can also be reached via a consideration of the market for claims, as was done in the simple case in the previous chapter. To the extent that the government runs a budget deficit, it must borrow to finance its expenditure; it is therefore necessary that saving shall be sufficient in amount to take up[1] these new debts the government must issue, as well as to finance the investment taking place (as seen in the previous chapter).

We can now turn to the other part of our subject matter—the consequences of changes in the government's tax or expenditure policy. Although this is a very important matter, particularly in relation to policy for stabilization of the economic system (of which more will be said in Chapter 5), the principles involved are so simple that we can deal with the matter quite quickly. If the government imposes additional taxes (as by increasing the rate of income tax in the pound), but does not spend them, it decreases the total amount of expenditure in the country on currently-produced goods and services: the people who have to pay the additional taxes reduce their consumption expenditure, but the government makes no corresponding increase in its expenditure. This leads to a chain of events very similar in character to those following a reduction in the level at which firms plan to invest; at the end of this process, there is a new equilibrium at a lower level of income, at which there is consistency between the plans of the various kinds of transactor. The reduction in the budget deficit (or the increase in the budget surplus) which is the immediate result of the increase in tax rates, leads to an inconsistency between plans. Although plans to save are reduced as a

---

[1] Either directly (e.g. purchase of government bonds) or indirectly through the intermediary of financial institutions (e.g. banks).

result of the higher taxes, they are not reduced by as much as the increase in taxes.[1] The result is that, if the increased taxes followed a period when income was in equilibrium, it is now found that planned saving exceeds the sum of planned investment and the planned budget deficit. As we found earlier, this inconsistency of plans is reconciled by a failure of some plans to be realized; for example, there might be unplanned investment by shopkeepers, if they find their their sales have been unexpectedly low. From here on, there develops the familiar chain of declining output and income, until incomes have fallen sufficiently for saving plans to be consistent with investment plans and the government's own plans for taxation and expenditure.

Exactly the same kind of argument can be used when the government makes other changes in its policies. For example, if it increases its expenditure on current output, while leaving tax rates unchanged, the effect is expansionary; the level of output and income rises and plans can only be consistent when incomes have risen sufficiently far. Again, a reduction of tax rates while government expenditure is unchanged is also expansionary, via the increased expenditure of households. Contrariwise, a reduction in government expenditure when tax rates are unchanged is a contractionary force.

[1] Except in the possible limiting case where the whole of the increased taxes are paid at the expense of a reduction in saving; but normally, as we have seen, the taxes will be partly at the expense of reduced consumption.

Chapter Four

THE LEVEL OF PRICES

UP to this point, we have avoided any consideration of changes in the general level of prices. We could do this, while remaining reasonably realistic, because of a widely-observed characteristic of most manufacturing countries in the twentieth century, to which we have already referred. This is the fact that when there is an appreciable amount of unemployment of men and machines, changes in demand for most manufactured goods lead to changes in the level of output of those goods, without any appreciable changes in their prices. A rise in demand for manufactured goods, in such conditions, is fully met by a rise in output, with the general level of prices remaining fairly constant. Similarly, falls in demand lead to falls in output but not to price falls. Of course, this is only a general tendency, but it is sufficiently general to be a valid basis for our theory. However, there are two major limitations to our generalization about price stability: it does not apply to primary products, and it does not apply to manufactured goods, once full employment conditions are approached or reached.

Generally speaking, the output of primary products can rarely be expanded in the short period; and quite frequently, it is also impossible to contract the output of these goods at short notice. The extreme cases arise in the case of many crops, where the decision to produce the crop is made long before it actually matures, and it is impossible to increase the output in this interval. Moreover, it is very unlikely that the output will not appear on the market at the due time, because the costs of harvesting and marketing are generally quite small in relation to total costs of production. Thus, except to the extent that stocks are carried over from year to year, the supply of many agricultural products cannot easily be varied in the short run.[1] This means that a change in demand cannot be met by a change in output in the short run, and so it must lead to a change in price.

Even in the case of mineral products, where the supply can be varied more easily in the short run, the position does not usually approach that which we have described in the case of manufactured goods. Technological conditions in general are such that additional output is normally only available at appreciably higher costs; as output rises, more and more difficult deposits are brought into production; and as output falls, the more difficult deposits are the first to be abandoned.

Once full employment is approached in a manufacturing economy, similar reactions appear. A rise in demand, after a certain point, can only be satisfied at increasing costs per unit of output. These increasing costs arise for two reasons. The first is technological.[2]

[1] In other words, the short-run elasticity of supply is very low.

[2] In common economic terminology, it is the operation of the law of diminishing returns.

As the level of full capacity operations is approached, producers find that they are having to overwork some of the factors of production because no further supply is available, at least in the short run (for example, only a fixed number of machines is available in a factory). Since increased output is only available by overworking the factor of production in fixed supply, it results in increasing costs per unit of output.

The second reason for increasing costs once full capacity working is reached is associated with trade union policy. While trade unions are usually successful in resisting cuts in money wages when there is substantial unemployment, they push for and are able to obtain increases in money wages when unemployment is low. They can do this because their bargaining position is stronger when labour is scarce. And in the labour market, as in all other markets, the principle holds that an excess in demand over supply usually leads to a rise in price (in this case a rise in wages).

The consequences of these cost increases is that, after unemployment has fallen below a certain percentage (which may be about 3 per cent. in present-day Britain or America), rises in demand for manufactured goods lead to rises in prices; only a part of the increased demand is satisfied by a rise in output. Furthermore, when unemployment falls to very low levels, no further rises in output are possible, and the sole effect of further rises in demand is that prices rise (or, alternatively, deliveries take longer). This extreme position may come about when unemployment falls to about $\frac{1}{2}$ per cent. There are some people who are unemployable, because they are incapable of adding anything to output. Moreover, there are always some people temporarily unemployed as they shift between jobs.

The zone in which a rise in demand leads to both price and output changes in a manufacturing economy is most important, because the level of unemployment which is widely held to be the maximum which is policitically desirable may well lie in this zone, which can be called the 'full employment zone'. When unemployment is extremely low, so that no rises in output from existing productive capacity are possible, we are in a purely inflationary zone.

Although the full employment zone is of the utmost importance, it is a little tricky to analyse, because two different kinds of change are to be found in it. Similarly, it is a little difficult to deal with the analysis of changes in demand in a primary producing country, where both prices and output alter. It is, therefore, convenient as a stage in the argument to ignore these mixed cases, and to consider circumstances where rises in the level of demand lead solely to price rises. This analysis applies either to a primary-producing economy where supply is quite inelastic, or to a fully-employed industrial economy. In the case of the latter, we can assume that up to full employment, rises in demand are met solely by rises in output; after this point, they lead solely to price rises. In other words, we are assuming that up to the point of full employment all increases in demand are fully met by increases in demand without any price changes, but as soon as 'full employment' is reached, the only effect of an increase in demand is to raise prices.

Another feature of full employment[1] has further important consequences. We have seen that a *rise* in demand, once full employment has been reached, leads to a rise in prices; but a subsequent fall in demand does not lead to falls in prices; instead it leads to falls in the level of output. The predominant reason for this is the fact already mentioned, that trade unions generally are successful in resisting wage cuts when there is unemployment, while they generally press for and receive increases in money wages when demand for labour is high in relation to supply. It follows that there is a sort of ratchet mechanism affecting prices: if the level of demand fluctuates around the full employment level, prices rise when demand is high and output falls when demand is low; prices do not fall back from each successively higher level which they reach. Of course, all this is subject to substantial modification to the (important) extent that primary products enter into the price level; but as a broad description of price changes in a manufacturing economy which is fluctuating appreciably around the full employment level, this analysis is reasonably valid.

A Purely Inflationary Situation

We now have to consider in more detail the range above full employment, in which pure inflation takes place. Here, fundamentally the same mechanisms operate as those we considered in our analysis of changes in the levels of output and activity in conditions

---

[1] Whether regarded as a point as we are doing (rather unrealistically) or as a range (which it is in reality).

of unemployment, in Chapter 3. We can conveniently start from a position where our economy was in equilibrium precisely at full employment, and is then disturbed by a rise in the level of fixed investment plans of firms (or of expenditure plans by the government). Exactly the same principles apply as earlier; the change means that transactors' plans are no longer consistent with one another, so that some plans are no longer precisely realized. This leads to a subsequent adjustment of plans, which further disturbs the situation. The only possible equilibrium is one where all plans are, once again, consistent. Such consistency cannot come about in this case through a series of rises in the levels of activity and real income; instead, it comes about (if it comes about at all) through a series of rises in prices and money incomes. For example, when firms find their stocks of finished goods declining unexpectedly (i.e. when unplanned disinvestment occurs) they can no longer react by raising output; instead, they raise prices. Inflation is simply this cumulative process of rising prices.

Two features of this process of change are significantly different from the multiplier process discussed earlier. One is that circumstances may be such that there is no possible equilibrium level of income; the price rises may go on indefinitely and may in fact get faster and faster. This is a possibility we shall discuss further a little later. The second is that we must take account of the possibility that different transactors may be affected by the inflationary process in very different ways. This can be seen by considering what happens to income recipients. In an expansionary multiplier process, of the kind discussed in the previous chapter, the households which adjusted their expenditure plans were all households which had been made better off by the expansionary[1] process; their money and real incomes rose, and consequently they increased their money and real expenditure. In the inflationary process, we have to consider the possibility of income recipients (households) being affected in three different ways.

In the first place, some households may enjoy an increase in the price of the things they sell (or which are sold by the firms in which they own shares), while the prices of the things they buy do not rise as much. Such households enjoy a rise in real income, and correspondingly, they will increase their real and their money expenditure. This case is parallel with that considered in our discussion of households' reactions in the multiplier process.

The second kind of effect arises in the case of households where money incomes and the prices of the things they buy happen both to go up by the same percentage. Real income is therefore constant. It is reasonable to suppose that such households will keep their real expenditure constant by raising both money expenditure plans and savings plans expressed in terms of money by the same percentage as the price and income rise. These households neither gain nor lose in the

---

[1] The expansionary multiplier process is the one with which parallels in the inflationary process should be drawn; there is no parallel sequence of cumulative price reductions to the sequence of output reductions in the contractionary multiplier process, for reasons that have already been considered.

process, but they do adjust their plans expressed in terms of money.

The third possible kind of household is the one which clearly *loses* as a result of the inflationary process: the prices of the things it sells rise less than the prices of the things it buys. As a consequence, the household can be expected to cut its real expenditure.

Here, then, is a new element, which does not exist in the expansionary multiplier process. In that process, households enjoy unexpectedly large incomes, while firms find their sales unexpectedly large—in no sense can this be regarded as a loss by either group of transactor. On the other hand, it is in the nature of inflation that there must inevitably be some losers somewhere. Inflation is the process of rising prices following an attempt to buy more goods and services than are available; temporarily the situation may be alleviated by stock reductions (unplanned disinvestment), but this can only be temporary, since stocks are exhaustible, and in any case firms are not likely to be willing to let their stocks run down indefinitely. There must, therefore, be losers, in the sense that there are those who are unable to obtain as many goods as they would have been able to obtain, in the absence of the inflationary price rises.

These losers may be of two kinds. As we have seen, they may be income recipients, whose money incomes do not rise as much as prices. Alternatively, they may be those transactors, such as firms, which are not income recipients but nevertheless make expenditures: they base their expenditure on borrowing. If a firm is borrowing at a rate of £100,000 a year and investing in plant at that rate, then if the price level doubles the amount of investment it is doing measured in real terms is halved. We can reasonably say that, in this respect, the firm (although clearly in a different position from the household) is 'losing' as a result of the inflation.

The new element which is introduced into the situation by the existence of 'losers' is that these transactors may try to defend themselves against these losses. For example, those households whose real incomes fall as a result of the inflationary process may refuse to supply the things they sell unless their real incomes are partially or wholly restored. Thus, trade unions may threaten to withdraw their members' labour unless wages rise sufficiently to make up for rises in the cost of living; and similarly business may be willing to sell only at prices sufficient to maintain the level of their profits in real terms. In this way, these households can try to maintain their real income and so their real expenditure. When a considerable number of transactors is making effective defensive reactions of this kind, we have a situation which is commonly described as 'cost inflation': the transactors concerned are refusing to accept the reductions in their real income and expenditure which would otherwise arise from the increase in the costs of the things they buy. Again, other transactors may make defensive reactions directly designed to maintain their real expenditure: if the firm in the preceding paragraph doubles its investment in money terms, to £200,000 per year, it is maintaining its level of investment in real terms.

Even though defensive reactions of this kind are frequently made and are frequently effective, the fact remains that there must be losers somewhere in an inflationary process. Each effective defensive reaction increases prices either directly or through increasing total demand (if not both); this pushes the inflationary process on its way and creates further losers. Quite possibly, defensive reactions that look as though they will be adequate turn out to be inadequate in fact; for example, labour may demand higher wages to allow for past increases in the cost of living, but still fail to restore real incomes because the higher wages themselves increase the cost of living still more. In any case, the important point is that defensive reactions speed up the process of inflation. Moreover, if all the transactors in an economy are acting defensively, and refuse to accept any reduction in their real incomes and/or expenditure (from the level which is in excess of what the economy can produce) then the process of inflation continues indefinitely. For example, if government expenditure is increased in an economy which is already at full employment, and then no transactor is willing to accept a reduction in his real income and/or real expenditure, there is a perpetual attempt to buy more goods and services than are available. As a result, prices rise indefinitely; at each stage some transactors find their plans are not realized, because of the effects of rising prices; consequently they adjust their plans in order to restore their real income and/or expenditure, and this causes further price rises.

Although defensive reactions by transactors can be

relied on to intensify the inflationary process, inflation can continue for a long time without any defensive reactions at all. A continuing process of price rises can result, simply because of a series of passive adjustments of plans to an initiating change of circumstances. For example, if the government raises its level of money expenditure in a fully employed economy, this leads to increased prices and so to increases in money incomes. Even if all households are, as a result, left just as well off as before in real terms (because prices and incomes have increased by the same percentage) households will adjust their plans in money terms. If my income was £10 and I consumed £9, and then all prices and my income double, then I will adjust my plans to consume £18. This additional money expenditure by households in turn causes further pressure of demand, which causes further price rises. These involve further rises in money incomes, and therefore further adjustments in plans. (This is an example of a situation commonly described as 'pure demand inflation.')

It may be noted that, as a matter of practical judgement, it may be impossible to tell whether a cumulative series of price rises involves truly defensive reactions or not. In the last case considered, each rise in prices and money incomes was the result of an excess of demand over supply; yet it might well seem that individual price and income rises within the process were purely the result of attempts by the transactors concerned to defend their real standard of living. For example, wage rises may be the *result* of excess of demand for labour over supply; but the excuse for

E

them might be the need to defend the workers' standard of living against the effects of price rises.

The Ending of Inflation

The necessary condition for the ending of inflation is quite a simple application of familiar principles. There can only be equilibrium in the level of prices if plans of transactors are consistent with one another. This can only be so if total plans for expenditure do not exceed total output. But, as we have seen, inflation is initiated and kept going by attempts to spend more, in real terms, than is available from current output. Therefore, inflation can only be brought to an end by the reduction in the real expenditure plans of some transactor or transactors.

This reduction can come about in either of two ways; real incomes may be reduced, with the consequent effect that real expenditure falls; or, alternatively, real expenditure may be reduced directly.

An example of the first mechanism may arise where some groups in the country are unable to defend themselves against the effect of rising prices on their incomes. For example, landlords may not be allowed to increase rents; therefore, as other prices and incomes rise, landlords' real income falls, and therefore their real expenditure falls. There is a redistribution of real income away from landlords towards the rest of society, and total real expenditure by landlords iffalls; this fall goes far enough, it may restore equilibrium in the economy as a whole.

An example of the automatic operation of the second

mechanism might arise if the inflation is caused by a rise in money expenditure by the government to a new level at which it is maintained constant throughout the inflation. As prices rise, this constant level of money expenditure becomes less and less in real terms, so that the excess of demand over supply of resources in the economy, measured in real terms, becomes less and less. This causes the price rise to slow down, and eventually to stop.

So far we have assumed that the process of inflation is not impeded by a shortage of money. But obviously an inflation cannot go on for long if the quantity of money is limited. If, for example, the government drastically limits the amount of money that is available, sooner or later transactors will find that there is less money available for carrying out their transactions than they consider desirable: as prices rise, the need for money for these purposes rises correspondingly, and if the supply is not allowed to expand in proportion, a shortage of money develops. If this shortage becomes serious enough, people hasten to sell goods and services in order to acquire bigger holdings of money, and these additional resources coming on to the market inhibit the price rises. Thus the limitation to the quantity of money will have stopped the inflation.

Although an inflation may come to an end of its own accord, it may, if the supply of money grows sufficiently fast, continue indefinitely at a steady rate. Indeed, it may very well accelerate, so that each year's percentage price rise is larger than in the preceding year. This is particularly likely to happen if inflation has gone on for long enough for people to expect it to continue. If this is the case, they are likely to intensify their attempts to defend their real incomes, as by demanding wage increases sufficient to allow for expected future price rises. To the extent that this happens, the process is accelerated. Moreover, once a general expectation of rising prices sets in, people will try to defend the real value of their wealth, by trying to switch out of holdings of money and assets whose value is fixed in terms of money, into assets whose value is likely to rise with the price level. One example of such assets is a share in a company: profits are likely to rise more or less in line with prices. Another example is real wealth; to the extent that this switch occurs, there may be additional demand for current output, and so additional pressure on prices. Similarly, people may try to take advantage of rising prices by buying up real wealth to sell at a higher price later; this additional stockbuilding also adds to pressure of demand.

If the acceleration of inflation goes far enough, the point is reached where prices rise hourly, and no one holds any more money than he can help, because it is losing its value so rapidly. This state of 'hyperinflation' has only been reached on a few occasions, usually in times of political disturbance after wars, but when it happens it can wreck the whole economic and social system.

Although it is perfectly possible for an inflationary situation to get right out of control in this way, such events are the exception rather than the rule. Much more likely to occur in practice is a persistent tendency for prices to creep upwards. This is more difficult to combat than a runaway inflation, because of the existence of the asymmetry around full employment that has already been noted. If demand is above the full employment level, prices rise; if demand falls below the full employment level, output falls and prices of manufacturers fall very little. Therefore, if activity is being kept on average at full employment, but is fluctuating to some extent around that level (as is almost unavoidable in practice), prices will tend to rise by a sort of 'ratchet' effect.

Fortunately, the situation is not perhaps quite as unsatisfactory as may seem, because full employment is not really reached precisely at any one point; it is better regarded as extending over a zone. As was pointed out earlier, there will usually be a range of activity in manufacturing economies within which a rise in demand leads to both price and output changes. In economies such as that of Britain and America, this range may be that between $\frac{1}{2}$ per cent. and 3 per cent. of unemployment.

The existence of this range means that an increase in demand at full employment levels does not push the economy straight into a purely inflationary situation, with no reactions other than a cumulative series of price rises. To some extent, inflationary processes do operate in the full employment zone; the cumulative process of rising prices is one element in the situation. But there are also other elements at work. For one thing, full capacity working is not likely to be reached simultaneously in all industries. When this situation is reached in some industries, wages and prices within those industries are likely to rise, while wages and prices elsewhere are still constant. The resulting rise of real incomes received by people in these industries is likely to attract some labour and other productive resources away from other industries, so increasing the potential capacity of the industries which had reached full capacity. In this case, the price rises are not cumulative, but make it possible for output to rise further. All these characteristics of the full employment *zone* suggest that an increase in demand at full employment, although causing some price increases, does not necessarily set off a rapid cumulative inflationary process.

Another common development in the full employment zone is for order books to lengthen in some industries that have reached full capacity. Such a development is only possible up to a certain point; but to the extent that it happens, it can prevent price rises from taking place.

Finally there is another powerful reason for some degree of optimism about the dangers of persistent tendencies to inflation. In an economy where productivity is rising rapidly, quite large rises in wages and other money incomes are consistent with price stability. This means that wage increases do not necessarily give rise to defensive reactions, because they do not necessarily bring about increases in the cost of living. If each of the firms in a country produces 5 per cent. more goods than in the preceding year and sells them at the same price per unit as previously, then the money incomes of the community rise by 5 per cent., even though prices have not risen at all. Thus, if productivity is rising sufficiently quickly, it is perfectly possible for people to enjoy substantial increases in money incomes each year, without corresponding price rises.

All this suggests that the dangers of inflation can easily be exaggerated. But it certainly does not imply that they are absent.

Chapter Five

ECONOMIC INSTABILITY AND
STABILIZATION POLICY

THE analysis of the preceding chapters suggests that one of the main practical problems of economic policy is the avoidance both of inflation and of unemployment. Once demand pushes into and beyond the full employment zone, there arises a tendency to a cumulative series of price rises, which may never come to an end of its own accord. It is, therefore, important that demand should not be allowed to rise so high that these conditions occur for long. At the same time, it is at least equally desirable to hold unemployment as low as possible. This means that conditions are always likely to be dangerously near to inflation.

Nor is this the only problem of economic stabilization. As is suggested by the preceding arguments, there is no reason why the economic system should show any automatic tendency to employ resources fully: it is perfectly possible that there may be long periods when the levels of income and output are well below full employment.

Nor is even this the end of the matter. Both experience and theory suggest that the normal course of events is for the level of income and activity to fluctuate quite substantially. Very broadly, it is possible to distinguish two kinds of fluctuations of this kind. On the one hand, there are fluctuations which do not involve very large changes in the level of activity, and which take two or three years to work round from one peak to the next. These short fluctuations seem to be largely associated with two things. In the first place, they are associated with changes in the level of stocks (or inventories) held by manufacturers and traders; if traders for any reason plan to increase their level of stocks of goods, a temporary surge in the level of activity is likely to result. The surge is only temporary, because the increased expenditure lasts only while the new level of stocks is being built up. Similarly, a temporary decline in the level of activity comes about if manufacturers and traders plan to reduce their level of stocks. In the second place, relatively short cycles in the level of activity can result from attempts by the government to stabilize the level of activity in the face of the inevitable changes that are always taking place in economic conditions. For example, if the economic situation has been allowed to get rather inflationary, and then the government comes in to impose restrictive measures in order to end the inflation, there is a real danger that the economy will, in the process, be pushed over into a situation of rather too much unemployment. This kind of fluctuation is particularly likely, if the government is slow in recognizing that the economic situation has moved away from equilibrium, if it is then also slow in doing anything to correct the situation, and if when it does take action, the government is impatient and tries to put things right too sharply. It is fairly obvious that such delayed and jerky reactions are hardly likely to lead to a smooth restoration of equilibrium.

The other kind of fluctuation in the level of activity is much more serious when it occurs, but it is very likely that it can be eliminated by appropriate stabilization policy by the government, whereas it seems very unlikely indeed that short cycles of the kind described in the preceding paragraph can be fully eliminated in any economy whose working depends on the co-ordination of the actions of many independent trans-actors. This more serious kind of fluctuation involves wide fluctuations in the level of activity and the length of time from one boom to the next may be of the order of ten years. This cycle is commonly known as the trade cycle, which was an important feature of the world economy from the Napoleonic Wars up to the Second World War. It may now have been mastered, as a result of the insight into economic processes which has been acquired in the last generation.

Many theories of the trade cycle have been deve-loped; none of them is by any means fully satisfactory and, indeed, it is most unlikely that any single theory can satisfactorily explain all the cycles that have been observed. All that will be attempted here is an outline of a theory which is almost certain to be an element in any plausible explanation of twentieth-century trade cycles, and which demonstrates the way in which major instability may easily develop in the economic system.

The basis of this theory is the interaction between the familiar multiplier process and the effects of changes in income on the level of fixed investment by firms. We have seen how a rise in the level of fixed investment by firms leads to a (multiple) rise in the level of income activity, assuming unemployed resources to be available. In addition to this familiar reaction, there is another which may operate: changes in income and activity may induce changes in the level of firms' plans to carry out fixed investment. When this happens, the chain of causation is linked round in a 'loop': investment affects income, which in turn affects investment plans.

Beofre looking at this process as a whole, it will be convenient to look at the unfamiliar part of the loop: the dependence of investment plans on income levels. The basis of this relationship is the simple technological fact that there will usually be some optimum relationship[1] between the level of output of a firm and the amount of fixed capital equipment the firm needs to produce that output. Perhaps £1,000 worth of equipment (machines, buildings, etc.) is needed to produce £500 of output per year, and £2,000 of equipment for £1,000 of output; in this case we can say that the optimum capital-output ratio for this firm is 2. If the firm finds that its actual capital-output ratio is other than the optimum,[2] it can be expected to try to correct the situation. If the actual ratio is less than the optimum the firm will probably try to install more capital equipment. If the actual ratio is greater than the optimum (so that some equipment is lying idle or is under-utilized) the firm is likely not to replace some of its equipment as it wears out.

[1] Given prices and the state of technological knowledge.
[2] For example because there has been an unexpected rise in sales and so in output.

At this point, the use of the distinction drawn in Chapter 2 between net and gross investment is necessary. Net investment takes place when firms are not merely replacing equipment as it wears out, but are installing additional equipment. If no additional equipment is being installed, but if equipment is being replaced as it wears out, we say that net investment is zero and that the only investment which is taking place is gross investment. Gross investment is equal to net investment plus replacement of fixed capital equipment, etc., as it wears out.

Using this terminology, it is apparent that the firm whose actual capital-output ratio is substantially more than the optimum is unlikely to carry out any investment, either gross or net. A firm whose capital-output ratio is at the optimum can be expected not to carry out any net investment, but will carry out sufficient gross investment to replace equipment as it wears out, so maintaining the optimum situation. Lastly, a firm whose actual capital-output ratio is less than the optimum can be expected to carry out positive net investment: it replaces equipment as it wears out and also adds to total equipment. If the firm's level of output is growing at a steady rate, its net investment will be constant; if output is growing 10 per cent. a year, the firm will wish to add 10 per cent. to its capital equipment, if it is to maintain its optimum capital-output ratio. If the level of output is growing at an accelerating rate (say 5 per cent. last year and 10 per cent. this year), then net investment will be increasing. On the other hand, if output is still growing but at a less rapid rate than in the past, its net investment will be declining.

Clearly, this is very likely to lead to economic instability. We can easily link this theory of the influence on investment plans of the relationship between the current level of output and the amount of capital equipment available with the theory of the multiplier; if we do so, we have a theory of the trade cycle.

It does not matter greatly where we break into the situation; a convenient starting point is a position where trade is much more depressed than it has been in the fairly recent past, so that most firms in the economy find that they have more capital equipment than is needed for producing their current level of output. As a result, most of them do not replace equipment as it wears out—gross investment is very low; for the purposes of the argument, we can assume it is zero.

This situation may continue for some time, but eventually, so much equipment will have worn out through age or use that the actual capital-output ratio is down to the optimum. At this point, a new element enters the situation: replacement becomes necessary as capital wears out. In other words, gross investment now starts.

In the familiar manner, this rise in the level of investment initiates an expansion of the level of income and activity, through the normal multiplier process. This in turn has the result that firms find they have less than the optimum amount of capital equipment for producing current levels of output. In other words, the capital-output ratio is below the optimum, and firms therefore start to plan net investment: they decide to add to the total amount of equipment they hold, and not merely to hold the amount stable. This reaction is an additional expansionary force in the stituation; the higher total level of investment accelerates the expansion in the level of income and activity that is already taking place. In turn, this makes still more net investment necessary, so that firms can catch up with the still higher level of output.

What we get, then, as a result of the 'loop' in the chain of causation, is that the increase in the level of investment leads to an increase in activity, which 'feeds back' and leads to a further increase in the level of investment. Observation of the real world suggests that this feedback is quite powerful, so that the expansionary process we have described contains no self-limiting forces within itself.

Nevertheless, there must be a limit to the possible expansion of output. This limit is provided by the full employment ceiling, where no more men are available to operate any new equipment and output cannot be expanded any further. This limit to the increase in output has an important influence on the course of events. Once output has reached its ceiling and firms realize that output is levelling out, they will make no further plans for adding to their capital equipment. As a result, plans for net investment fall away sharply; the only investment plans which continue to be made after the level of output has flattened out at the full employment level are plans for gross investment: firms continue to replace equipment as it wears out, but do not plan to add to their total equipment.

This position, at the top of the cycle, is, however, extremely unstable. The sharp decline in total investment, which occurs when net investment plans fall away to zero, initiates a contraction in the level of income and activity, in the familiar manner. But this in turn means that firms find their actual capital-output ratio greater than the optimum. Gross investment therefore also falls away sharply. This accelerates the contractionary process, and the only possible equilibrium position is one where income has fallen sufficiently for (gross) savings plans to be equal to (gross) investment plans. At this point, a period of temporary stability is reached, because firms find themselves with considerably more capital equipment than is the optimum for producing the current (low) level of output. Until sufficient capital equipment has worn out for the actual capital-output ratio to decline to the optimum, gross investment will be zero and stagnation of the level of income and output continues. Eventually, however, the actual capital-output ratio does fall to the optimum; replacement starts again and initiates the upswing.

It cannot be claimed that the sequence of events considered above gives an adequate explanation of the trade cycle. All the same, it does indicate the kind of instability that can easily be built up in the economic system. Correspondingly, a heavy burden is placed on the government, in its attempts to stabilize the level of income and activity at full employment.

The general characteristics of the stabilization policies which can be used by governments (in countries predominantly concerned with manufacturing and with no foreign trade) are quite simple. What is necessary is that forces should be set in operation which lead to economic expansion if the level of activity is currently (or is forecast to be) below full employment levels. Conversely, forces leading to economic contraction should be set into operation if the level of prices is currently rising or is expected to rise in the near future. The aim, in other words, is to maintain full employment without rising prices. Broadly speaking, this is the policy aim which is supported by most political groups in the advanced industrialized countries, although there are differences about the precise meaning of this policy aim. For example, some people are more fearful of the risks of inflation than others; for some, inflation is the worse evil, for others, unemployment is the worse. And as we have already seen, there is to some extent a conflict between the aims of full employment and stable prices.

There are three main kinds of instrument that can be used to help bring about economic stabilization in a closed economy. They are fiscal controls, direct controls, and monetary controls. Fiscal controls are imposed by means of the government's taxation and expenditure policy, whose effects were discussed in Chapter 3. Direct controls are imposed by instructions from the government forbidding (or occasionally compelling) other transactors to do something. Monetary controls operate through the market for claims, as through the rate of interest and the banking system (which we shall discuss more extensively in subsequent chapters). Their effects on conditions in the markets

for goods and services operate via conditions in the
market for claims.

The choice between these three kinds of control
depends to an important extent on political judgements,
but they do vary substantially in their purely economic
effects, so it will be convenient briefly to discuss the
main differences.

The principles lying behind the use of fiscal controls
should be apparent from the earlier discussion of the
effect of the government on the level of activity. For
example, if government expenditure is increased or if
taxation is reduced, the consequence will be a rise in the
level of activity. Such policies can always have very big
effects on the level of activity, if they are politically
acceptable: for example, a sufficiently large budget
deficit can, in time, always bring the level of activity up
to full employment. In practice, however, there may
be difficulties. For example, budget deficits (or surpluses) may not be regarded as desirable. In particular,
it used often to be held that the government should act
like a prudent household, and never get into debt, even
to buy fixed capital equipment. The only justification
for this argument is that *excessive* budget deficits inevitably lead to inflation. Another, more real, difficulty
is that for political reasons it is often not easy to change
taxes when this might be desirable from the point of
view of economic stability; and it may also be difficult
to make rapid changes (especially downwards) in the
level of government expenditure. These difficulties tend
to lead to the further one, that fiscal controls are frequently rather slow in their action; a difficulty which

F

is enhanced by the convention of annual budgets.

Direct controls consist of instructions and orders to firms and households, such as building licensing and rationing. To people of some political views these controls are all and always undesirable; other people seem to like them simply for their own sake. Such controls are almost always negative in form, telling someone not to do something; this means that they can be brought into operation very quickly. In practice, however, it may be considered equitable to allow people to carry out existing commitments, and then these controls are slower in operation (though probably still faster than fiscal controls). A further characteristic of direct controls is that they can easily be used in a discriminatory manner; for example, house building may be allowed but building of shops restricted.

Monetary controls were long regarded as the only respectable kind of control. They can operate in two ways: they may operate through changes in the rate of interest, or they may operate through affecting the willingness of banks to lend. How these effects can be brought about will be discussed in Chapters 6–9. If the rate of interest changes, this may affect the willingness of transactors to save and invest. If interest rates rise, a bigger income is received by anyone who saves and purchases an interest-bearing security; this effect may persuade some people to save more. Again (and this effect is probably more important) a rise in the rate of interest may discourage some transactors from borrowing and investing (either in fixed equipment or in stocks of goods). The effects of interest rates on investment plans can easily be exaggerated. Traders' investment in stocks are probably influenced mainly by other forces (which will be considered in the next chapter). Only if the willingness of bankers to lend is altered by monetary policy is there likely to be much influence on traders' holdings of stocks. The rate of interest only has substantial influence on capital charges on fixed assets if the latter are long-lived. Total capital charges include provision for depreciation as well as interest payments; if capital equipment is bought with the proceeds of a loan, allowance has to be made for the replacement of the equipment when it wears out or for the repayment of the loan; otherwise there is no continuing asset to offset a continuing debt. If the rate of interest is 4 per cent. and a machine costing £1,000 is to be written off over five years, total capital charges per year are £40 interest plus £200 depreciation provisions. If the rate of interest now doubles to 8 per cent. capital charges only increase by £40, to a new total of £280; the increase in total capital charges is relatively quite small. The effects of interest rate changes would have been much greater if the machine were to be written off over fifty years; the annual depreciation charges would be only £20, and total capital charges would rise from £60 to £100 with a doubling of the rate of interest from 4 per cent. to 8 per cent. Only in the case of really long-lived investments (such as houses and railways) are changes in the rate of interest likely to have big effects on investment plans. But since long-lived investments frequently take a long time to plan and carry out, the effects of monetary controls through interest rate changes are probably quite slow in their operation.

In addition to having to decide which stabilization instruments they are to use, the government must decide how strongly to use its chosen instrument or instruments, in order to maintain stability in the face of changing circumstances, or if that is not feasible, in order to restore it as quickly as possible. To the extent that the government can *forecast* changing economic circumstances with accuracy it is sensible to act on them and try to see that no disturbances arise. Some approach to this ideal is no doubt possible in practice, but it is certainly impossible to attain a sufficiently high degree of accuracy in forecasting economic events, for this approach to be sufficient by itself. It is, therefore, necessary for the government to react as appropriately as is possible to disturbances in the economic situation as soon as they appear. What is meant by 'appropriately' in these circumstances is a difficult question to answer. All that can be said simply is that it is essential to act as quickly as possible and it is desirable that action should not be too jerky. If action is taken quickly, the situation is not likely to have got far out of hand before something is done. If corrective action is not too jerky, it is likely that equilibrium will be regained reasonably smoothly, without serious oscillations on the way.

Chapter Six

WEALTH HOLDING AND THE RATE OF INTEREST

In the initial stages of this study, we explained that it would be convenient to separate decisions about additions to wealth holding from decisions about the form in which existing wealth shall be held. In the previous four chapters, we have been largely concerned with the consequences of changes in decisions about additions to wealth, such as changes in saving and investment plans. It is now necessary to switch to the other question, and to consider some of the major determinants of decisions about the form in which existing wealth shall be held, and some of the consequences of changes in those decisions.

There are two main reasons why this part of economic analysis can, within limits, conveniently be treated in isolation. One (which has already been mentioned) is that the total amount of wealth handed down from the past is large in relation to each week's or each year's additions to total wealth held; the stock of wealth handed down from the past has, therefore, a very large potential weight in the markets for different kinds of wealth. The second reason is that many wealth-holders do in fact switch their wealth between different kinds of asset, in particular between different kinds of claim; this has as a consequence the fact that a very large part of the total activity in the markets for many kinds of asset arises from switching of the form in which wealth-holders keep their assets. This means that the large potential weight arising from the existence of a great deal of old wealth is frequently brought to bear in these markets.

It has already been seen, in Chapter 1, that transactors choose to hold wealth because it will give them some kind of return. Transactors' decisions about the form in which to hold wealth are determined by the returns they believe they can get from the different kinds of wealth they might own. Our next concern is to look into the forces influencing transactors' views of these returns.

Decisions about the Form in which Wealth is Held

In the first place, it is obvious that if there are costs involved in holding a particular kind of wealth, these must be subtracted from the *gross* return on the wealth, to obtain the estimate of the *net* amount the transactor will get from holding that wealth. Most real assets involve such carrying costs; machines and stocks of many commodities deteriorate with time and need maintenance, shelter, and insurance. On the other hand, most claims (including money, bonds, and shares) do not involve appreciable carrying costs; at most they need a safe storing place, which is quite inexpensive for pieces of paper, however valuable they may be.

Leaving aside these negative returns, in the form of carrying costs, we can now consider the different ways in which an asset may give its owner positive returns.

Broadly speaking, we can distinguish three ways in which returns may accrue—an asset may give a '*yield*', it may give a return in the form of *convenience*, or it may give a return of *certainty*.

Many kinds of wealth gives a 'yield' of some kind or other. This may accrue in the form of a flow of money income, as is the case with wealth held as a bond or a share. Again, it may accrue in the form of physical output, that can be sold for more than the cost of the input; a common example is the yield given by the ownership of a machine. Again, the yield may arise because the money value of the asset increases with time; I may be able to buy something (perhaps a ton of copper or a government bond) for £100 today and sell it for £110 next month.

The ownership of many kinds of asset gives substantial returns in terms of convenience. It is convenient to own at least part of your wealth in the form of things which you are likely to need in the near future, or in the form of things which can easily be changed into things you will need in the near future. Thus a firm will hold stocks of raw materials, for the convenience of having them ready to use when they are needed; it is almost intolerably difficult to plan production if raw materials are only arriving in the factory at the moment when they are needed. Again, a shop holds stocks of goods on its shelves, because it is more convenient to receive bulk deliveries and because it can be prepared for unexpectedly large sales. Or a bank can be expected to hold stocks of coins and notes in its tills, ready to pay out on demand to its depositors.

This motive of convenience is particularly important in the case of decisions to hold money. It is convenient for a firm or an individual to hold some wealth in the form of money, because money can be used immediately to buy anything available for sale. If I hold wealth in shares or savings certificates, they are not much use to me if I want to buy a loaf of bread, whereas money can be immediately exchanged for bread, without trouble or expense.

Closely associated with the motive of convenience is the motive of certainty. Broadly speaking, those forms of wealth which possess the attribute of convenience also enjoy that of certainty. This is so, for example, in the case of stocks of raw materials held by manufacturers: the convenience of owning such stocks largely derives from the certainty enjoyed by the manufacturer about the ability to keep production going, and not to be interrupted by a shortage of materials. Similarly, there is the certainty enjoyed by the owner of money that he will be able to buy anything he wants which is for sale.

If a transactor is quite sure what kind of commodity he will want to use in the relatively near future, he is sensible if he acquires a stock of the commodity, ready to use. He then receives benefits in the forms of convenience and certainty. If, on the other hand, a transactor is unsure what commodities he will want even in the quite near future, it is not sensible for him to acquire a stock of commodities. Again, if he thinks he may want to buy and use services in the near future, he cannot acquire a stock of them ready to use, because they cannot be stored. In either of these cases, it is by holding money that a transactor can most easily obtain the benefits of convenience and certainty. With money, it is possible to buy anything. Moreover, there is the important fact that (at least for relatively short periods of time) prices in general are relatively stable in terms of money. The prices of many individual commodities and claims can vary substantially in quite short periods of time. Therefore, such ways of holding wealth are rather unsatisfactory to a person who is unsure what he will want. If I am not reasonably sure about exactly what goods I shall need in the near future, it is sensible to satisfy the needs for certainty and convenience in one's wealth by holding money. This preference is often described as a preference for liquidity: money is the most liquid of assets. In other words, it most satisfactorily combines the qualities of convenience and certainty.

Each of these various influences on decisions about the form in which wealth shall be held are to some extent relevant to all forms of wealth and to all kinds of transactor. Nevertheless, some are much more closely related to certain kinds of wealth and transactor than are others.

As an example, by far the most important determinants of decisions about holding wealth in the form of machines are the yield earned by the machine and its carrying costs. In the case of a bond or share, the yield is once again the most important determinant; in the cases of these kinds of wealth, the yield may come in either or both of two ways, and account must be taken of both of them. It comes partly in the form of interest earned on a bond or the dividends received by a shareholder. It also comes partly in the form of any rise in the market value of the share that may occur. Alternatively, of course, there is a reduction in total income or even a net loss if there is a fall in the market value of a bond or share.

In the case of wealth held in the forms of money and of stocks of goods, the most important determinants are the motives of convenience and certainty. A firm may be willing to hold bigger stocks of goods for other reasons; for example their carrying costs may fall as a result of falling insurance charges, or a yield may be expected from holding them because their price is going to rise. But in general, the main motives are convenience and certainty. Again, in the case of money, these two motives are the most important, although others may be relevant; for example, if the prices of practically all goods are expected to fall sharply, people may choose to hold more money than usual, because the power of a given quantity of money to buy goods is increasing.

It is fairly clear that the likelihood of switching between the holding of different kinds of wealth varies substantially with the kind of wealth that is held. The ultimate decisions about firms' holding of machines and stocks of goods, operating through the various determinants considered above, are the forces we have already discussed in earlier chapters. In particular, there can be little doubt that the main forces deciding holdings of these kinds of assets are, as we have already seen, linked with changes in the level of activity. On the other hand, there is much more to be said about the substantial switches which are likely between transactor's holdings of bonds, bills, shares, and money, as the relative attractiveness of these different kinds of claim varies. Any holder of wealth in one of these forms can easily and quickly switch his wealth into one of the others; and since there is a great deal of wealth in these forms handed down from the past, such switches have a predominant effect on demand and supply conditions in markets for bonds, bills, and shares.

It should be emphasized, however, that these switches are by no means the only influences. At least two others have to be borne in mind. One arises from the fact that, in a growing economy, saving and investment will be taking place continuously, and they will generally be accompanied by the acquisition of new claims by savers (in forms such as new issues of shares or bonds or newly-created money). The other important influence is that purely financial operations can take place. For example, the issuer of one kind of claim may withdraw it and issue another kind—e.g. a government may pay off bills by issuing bonds. Again, two transactors may simultaneously create two equal claims, one against the other; for example, if a bank gives me a loan, it creates a deposit for me (which is a new claim against the bank, owned by me) and at the same time a debt from me to the bank is created (i.e. a new claim against me, owned by the bank).

It will shortly be necessary to take account of the kinds of influence outlined in the preceding paragraph. As a first stage in the argument, however, it is simpler just to discuss the conditions determining the demand for the various kinds of claim, on the assumption that the amount of each in existence is fixed.

The general principles that apply are very similar to those in operation in the determination of the equilibrium level of income. There can only be a position of equilibrium if each wealth-holder is content with his situation; otherwise, he can be expected to try to improve his situation which will in turn disturb the situation of other people. In other words, there can only be equilibrium if each claim has a willing holder, and if there are no wealth holders who would prefer to hold something different from what they are holding.

The implications of this can easily be seen if we look for a moment solely at the market for shares, assuming (unrealistically) that it is completely isolated from the markets for all other kinds of claim. If there are some people who are currently holding say I.C.I. shares, but who would prefer, at present market prices, to hold say B.P. shares, and if everyone else is content with his position, the situation is not an equilibrium situation. The solution is simple and is rapidly brought about by market forces. The price of I.C.I. shares tends to fall and the price of B.P. shares tends to rise, and this goes on until everyone is a willing holder of whatever kind of share he has; the process of adjustment may well involve sympathetic movements in the prices of many other shares, until a new equilibrium is reached. In the new equilibrium, some people will have been persuaded to take up the I.C.I. shares because of the fall in their price; similarly, some people will have given up B.P. shares, because of the rise in their price.

It is now necessary to consider why some wealth-holders are willing to shift away from shares which get dearer, and into shares which are getting cheaper. There are two major reasons, which are closely linked with one another. If people see no reason to revise their views about the size of the dividends that will be distributed to shareholders at the end of the year then the fall in the share's price means that the ratio of the prospective dividend to the current purchase price of the share has risen. Measured in terms of prospective income yields the return from the share has risen. The second reason why people can be expected to switch towards holding shares that have become cheaper is that if the price of a share falls sufficiently far, many people will think the fall has overreached itself and the likelihood is that the more people will expect that the next price change will be a rise. This is not inevitably so; price falls may, up to a point, induce fear of further price falls. Moreover, all such speculation about future prices of shares depends largely on estimates of future dividend distributions, and market opinion about these will always be changing. In fact, a generalized description of the speculative forces in a market like the stock exchange is very complicated and beyond a point it is not very helpful. What is undoubtedly true, however, is that these speculative forces are of predominant importance on the stock market and that there is always some possible equilibrium in the market, at which each wealth-holder will be content with his position. Moreover, this equilibrium is always approached quickly, because it is easy to shift very quickly out of one share into another; on the other hand, the equilibrium is always shifting because circumstances and expectations are always changing.

The Determination of the Rate of Interest

Exactly the same kind of analysis to that just followed applies in the case of shifts between all kinds of asset. In practice, wealth-holders have a very wide range of choice; to make the argument more manageable, however, it is easier to consider choices between pairs of assets. From the point of view of economic theory one of the most important choices of this kind is that between interest-bearing securities and money. This relationship provides the most important element in the theory of the determination of the rate of interest; it also has the considerable virtue that it indicates the way in which speculative forces work in all asset markets, while at the same time being relatively simple to handle conceptually, particularly if we assume there is only one kind of interest-bearing security, namely the bond.

What we shall be concerned with here is the determination of the rate of interest at any moment of time. It is necessary as a preliminary to this to consider the nature of the rate of interest and the reasons why people pay it. The rate of interest is simply the percentage of the amount of a loan which borrowers have to pay each year to lenders. Borrowers are willing to pay interest because they believe they can use the loan for worthwhile purposes—typically for buying capital equipment or stocks of goods. Broadly speaking, then, interest is paid because loans can be put to productive purposes; the fundamental element lying behind the payment of interest is the productivity of capital; moreover, these forces of productivity undoubtedly affect the general level around which the rate of interest fluctuates. It can usually be expected that interest rates will tend to be high where capital is scarce in relation to the possible uses to which it can be put. All the same, this relationship is not very close, particularly in the medium and short run.

The main determinants of the rate of interest at any moment of time are the facts that in equilibrium all assets must be held by willing holders, and that switching only takes a very short time. If we confine ourselves to the choice between interest-bearing claims (bonds) and money, this amounts to saying that all existing bonds and all existing money must be willingly held by its present owners. If some people who are holding money would prefer to hold bonds, they will shift into bonds; the resulting increase in demand raises their price. But the price of existing bonds and the rate of interest necessarily vary inversely with one another. If the price of a piece of paper giving a claim to £5 a year should rise from £50 to £100, the rate of interest has fallen from 10 per cent. ($\frac{5}{50}$) to 5 per cent. ($\frac{5}{100}$); anyone who bought that piece of paper at its old, lower, price enjoyed an annual income of 10 per cent. of the price he paid, whereas anyone who buys it at its new, higher, price enjoys an annual income of only 5 per cent. of the price he pays. A rise in the price of bonds is, therefore, a fall in the rate of interest. Our argument so far amounts to saying that if some people who are holding money would prefer to hold bonds, the rate of interest will fall. Correspondingly, a swing the other way leads to a rise in the rate of interest.

The usual consequence of a rise in the price of bonds is a decrease in the willingness of people to hold them. The mechanism at work is very similar to that already considered in the case of share prices. For one thing, a rise in bond prices—i.e. a fall in interest rates— involves a lower annual income for anyone buying the bond at the higher price. This is, in itself, some discouragement to purchasers. In addition, purely speculative forces are extremely important in the market for bonds. Generally speaking, it can be expected (just as with shares) that the higher bond prices rise, the more people will come to expect that the next movement will be downwards. This means that people will usually become more reluctant to hold bonds. If I expect that the price of a bond yielding me £4 a year in income is going to fall from say £80 to £70 in the next year, I make a net loss of £6 during the year. I would, therefore, do better to get rid of the bond at its present price of £80 and hold something which will either give me a positive total yield, or which at least will retain its value, even if it provides no yield.

This second alternative is the one which a wealth-holder can be expected to follow, if the prices of all the income earning claims in which he is interested are tending to fall substantially. In these circumstances, he is likely to shift his wealth into money; this is an asset which gives no yield in the form of income, but which is certain in value as long as inflation is not too serious and which has the virtues of convenience and of having no carrying costs. Thus, when a wealth-holder expects the rate of interest to rise substantially, he is likely to want to hold more money than usual: he has an unusually strong preference for liquidity. This is the speculative motive for holding money: it arises from the belief that holding bonds (or other interest-bearing assets) is likely to lead to losses, so that it is safer to hold something whose money value is assured.

These speculative shifts between bonds and money account for what is probably the major determinant of the rate of interest at any moment of time.[1] The rate of interest (i.e. the price of bonds) must be such that wealth-holders are willing to hold precisely the existing number of bonds and precisely the existing amount of money. But at low rates of interest (high bond prices) very many people want to hold money for speculative reasons and relatively few to hold bonds; at high rates of interest (low bond prices) few people will want to hold money for speculative reasons and most will be willing to hold bonds, because few people will expect further substantial falls in bond prices. Clearly, there must be some intermediate point at which all the bonds in existence are held by willing holders and there are no people who hold money but would prefer to hold bonds. Where exactly this point lies depends on the

---

[1] In the absence of an active central banking policy, such as will be discussed in Chapters 7–9.

G

quantity of bonds and the quantity of money available
for these speculative purposes.

The amount of money which is available for speculative purposes is largely dependent on the quantity of
money in existence. The more money there is, the more
will be available (if other things are equal) for speculative holdings. But in fact other things are not equal.
Most money is used, for reasons of convenience and
certainty, to cover normal day-by-day and month-by-
month needs for carrying out transactions; money is
held because it is the most convenient and certain way
of holding wealth between the time of the receipt of
income and the use of that income for various kinds of
expenditure. This demand for money, dependent upon
the so-called 'transactions motive', can reasonably be
assumed to vary in direct proportion with the level of
income.

This relationship has important consequences. If
the level of income in a country rises, the need for
money for these transactions purposes rises in step.
But if the total quantity of money should happen to be
constant, this means that less is left over to satisfy
speculative demands to hold money. If the quantity of
bonds in existence has also remained unchanged, this
means that there has been a decline in the quantity of
money available for speculative holdings, relatively to
the quantity of bonds in existence. In order that
equilibrium may be restored in the market for claims,
the price of bonds must fall somewhat; then some people
will switch from speculative holdings of money, towards bonds, so releasing money needed for increased

transaction holdings. All this amounts to saying, therefore, that the rate of interest usually tends to rise if the level of activity rises while the quantity of money is unchanged.

In a similar manner, it can be seen that a change in the total quantity of money or bonds in existence, at a given level of income and activity, will also be likely to affect the rate of interest. If, for example, the government repurchases some of the bonds it has issued, paying out money for them, the quantity of bonds in the hands of the public falls and the quantity of money rises. The only possible equilibrium (when all other things are unchanged) is one where interest rates have fallen (bond prices have risen) sufficiently for the public to be willing to hold a bigger proportion of its wealth in the form of money and a smaller proportion in bonds.

Up to this point, the analysis has simply considered shifts between different kinds of shares and between bonds and money. In addition, it is necessary to consider the relationships between other pairs of assets. For example, wealth-holders commonly shift between bonds and shares; both provide a yield and involve no carrying costs, and so both are to a considerable extent similar to character. Because of this similarity, there is frequently a tendency for bond and share prices to move together; if the price of the one rises while the other is unchanged, some people may well switch from the one which has become dearer and so raise the price of the other; their motivations are similar to those already outlined in the cases of other shifts. Similarly, some borrowers may shift towards the kind of borrowing that has become cheaper.

It should be remembered, however, that there is an important difference between bonds and shares. The annual income yield on a bond is fixed in terms of money, whereas the income yield on a share fluctuates, as the firm changes its profit distributions from year to year. This has two consequences. In the first place, profits are likely to be higher in prosperous times than in bad times, and as a consequence, so are dividend distributions. Therefore, share prices tend to be high in good times and low in bad, while there is no reason why bond prices should move as much. In fact, bond prices may well move in the opposite direction, largely because the monetary authorities frequently use high interest rates (i.e. low bond prices) to restrain a boom. The second set of circumstances in which bond prices and share prices do not necessarily move sympathetically is when considerable inflation is expected. The income yield on bonds is fixed in terms of money, so that its real value falls in an inflation; on the other hand, profits are likely to rise in line with prices in general, so that shareholders' incomes are likely to be reasonably stable in real terms. There is, therefore, likely to be particularly heavy pressure to buy shares and to sell bonds when inflation is expected—share prices are then high and bond prices low.

The other pair of assets with which we can usefully concern ourselves are bonds and bills. Both of these provide an interest yield which is fixed in terms of money for the duration of the contract; the difference

between them lies in the duration of the contract.
A bill matures within a period of not more than a year
(usually three months) so that its owner can be sure of
the capital sum he owns in quite a short time; short-
term securities are relatively capital-certain. In this
respect, their qualities approach those of money; a bill
is intermediate in qualities between a bond and money.
It provides some yield, and to that extent it is like a
bond; it has a fairly certain value, and to that extent
it is like money.

Since bills and bonds are to quite a considerable
extent similar, there is a strong tendency for their prices
to move sympathetically. If interest rates on bonds rise
while interest rates on bills remain unchanged, some
people will switch from holding bills to holding bonds;
they get a bigger yield and they may very well speculate
on the likelihood of subsequent falls in long-term
interest rates. Similarly, debtors may try to switch
from issuing bonds to issuing bills. All these forces will
tend to cause short-term (bill) interest rates to rise in
sympathy with the rise in long rates.

In practice, the situation is that there is a whole
range of different assets, starting with money and
finishing with very long-dated (or undated) bonds;
the example of a bill is simply one case of an asset part
way along this spectrum. Broadly speaking, the position
is that if the general level of interest rates on the various
kinds of interest-bearing security are equal (looked at
over a longish period of time), the majority of wealth-
holders will prefer to hold relatively short-dated assets
(e.g. bills) while the majority of debtors will prefer to

issue long-dated securities (e.g. bonds). This is quite understandable; if wealth-holders can get the same income yield from holding bills, and can at the same time enjoy a high degree of certainty about the value of their capital, they are likely, in general, to prefer this situation to that of getting the same average income yield from holding bonds, and suffering uncertainty about the value of their capital. On the other hand, debtors are likely to prefer to know exactly what their commitments are, when they borrow for a long time; if they issue bonds they know exactly how much interest they will have to pay each year, whereas if they issue bills and keep renewing them as they mature, the amount they have to pay in interest each year fluctuates with the short-term rate of interest.

Since, therefore, there would be a preponderance of short-term borrowers and long-term lenders if long- and short-term interest rates were generally at the same level, the general level of long-term rates is higher than the general level of short rates. This persuades more wealth-holders to hold long-term securities and some debtors to issue short-term rather than long-term claims. At particular times, short-term interest rates may well be higher than long: short rates are more volatile than long, because they are more strongly influenced by immediate circumstances. On average, however, twentieth-century experience has generally been for short rates to be lower than long.

The divergence between the level of short- and long-term rates gives opportunities for making profit to various kinds of financial institutions, which are capital intermediaries, borrowing from their creditors and lending to other people. For example, building societies act as capital intermediaries who borrow short and lend long; they cover their costs and make a profit out of the differences between the rates at which they borrow and those at which they lend. In doing this, they tend to bring the general level of short-term interest rates nearer to the general level of long-term rates, because these institutions throw more weight than there would otherwise be on to total supply in the market for short-term claims and on to total demand for long-term claims.

Much the most important kind of financial institution doing this work of capital intermediary is the ordinary commercial bank, whose debts (its customers' deposits) are withdrawable on demand or at very short notice, and whose assets largely consists of claims which are likely to vary in value (e.g. bonds) or which are in practice not easily realizable (e.g. the loans they have made to their customers). The existence of such institutions tends to bring short- and long-term interest rates closer together than they would otherwise be, and for that reason alone they are important. But the economic significance of banks is much greater than this fact alone, and it is therefore necessary to give them extensive treatment.

Chapter Seven

BANKING PRINCIPLES

THERE are two main kinds of banking institution: commercial banks and central banks. Historically, the former developed first; they are the institutions with which most individuals and firms deal. Central banks are institutions which have particularly close relations with the government; their main function is to control the banking system and so to influence the overall economic situation of the country. This chapter considers the broad principles on which these two kinds of institution work.

The most important feature distinguishing banks (both central and commercial) from other financial institutions and from ordinary firms and households is that their debts are used as money. In modern economies, nearly all the money in circulation consists of a debt, either of a commercial bank or of the central bank. In Britain, the only other money which circulates today is the small change (from farthings up to half-crowns) which is issued by a Government Department (the Royal Mint).

Bank money is of two main kinds—bank notes and bank deposits. The former (of which the English pound note, issued by the Bank of England, is an example) is a piece of paper which can be passed from hand to hand and is generally accepted in payment of debts. As we saw in Chapter 1, the words on a pound note, 'I Promise to pay the Bearer on Demand the sum of One Pound', are now a complete anachronism. In the past, however, the statement was meaningful; the holder of a Bank of England note could, before 1914, demand its conversion into golden sovereigns, and the gold in a sovereign was itself worth one pound. Today, however, the 'intrinsic' value of practically all money is negligible; the paper on which a pound note is printed is worth almost nothing, but the note is worth a pound because it is generally accepted as money within the United Kingdom.

The other kind of money consists of bank deposits. They are simply a debt of a bank to its customer (the depositor) which is recorded in the bank's accounts. These deposits are of two main kinds: demand deposits[1] and time deposits.[2] The former are always convertible into bank notes on demand by the depositor; if I have a demand deposit I can withdraw any or all of it at a moment's notice. I can also, by giving instructions to the bank on a cheque, transfer any or all of my demand deposit to any person I may name. In the case of time deposits, I can do these things only after giving an agreed notice (usually one to three weeks) to the bank, stating my intentions.

It is possible for both central and commercial banks to create both of these kinds of money. In England, however, none of the commercial banks issues bank notes; the Bank of England (the central bank) issues all

[1] Also known as 'current account deposits'.

[2] Also known as 'deposits on deposit account'.

the notes which circulate. At the same time, the Bank of England does not do any substantial banking business with ordinary firms or households, so that practically all the bank deposits owned by the general public are held with the commercial banks. On the other hand, the Bank of England does act as banker, both to the government and to the other banks (including many overseas banks, as well as the English and Scottish commercial banks).

It may be noted that in other countries and at other times different arrangements may operate. Thus, the Scottish commercial banks still have a right of note issue, and in the first half of the nineteenth century most English banks issued notes. Again, in the United States, commercial banks bank with one another, and the government banks with various commercial banks; in both these respects, conditions there are different from those in Britain. In the arguments of the rest of this chapter, it will be convenient, and not misleading, to assume conditions like those in present-day England.

The fact that the debts of banks are used as money accounts for the central importance of banks in the financial mechanism. It means that, whenever a bank increases its total debts, the total amount of money in circulation in the country increases. Banks act as *creators of money*. Thus, if a bank (either a commercial bank or a central bank) buys a government bond from a member of the general public and pays for it, either with a bank deposit or with bank notes, then the total amount of money in the hands of the general public rises. Similarly, if a bank makes a loan to a member of the public, creating a deposit in his favour, the amount of money in circulation rises.[1] In both these cases, there is a process by which the bank exchanges claims with a member of the public; in the first case, the bank acquires a claim in the form of a bond and the member of the public acquires a claim against the bank in the form of a note or a deposit; in the second case, the bank acquires a claim against the borrower for subsequent repayment of the loan, and the borrower acquires a claim against the bank in the form of a deposit. The basic significance of both of these transactions is that the new claim acquired by the member of the public is money.

In the course of these transactions, banks are carrying out the work of *capital intermediaries*, which was mentioned at the end of the previous chapter. They provide a mechanism by which wealth-holders can own much of their wealth in a form possessing the attributes of convenience and certainty, while debtors can owe debts which they do not have to repay at a moment's notice, and which may not be repayable for years.

Moreover, in carrying out all these operations, banks carry out their other major function, namely that of the '*ledger clerk*' who sperates a large part of the country's payments system. It is convenient to make large payments by cheque rather than bank notes; in these transactions, banks carry out the function of transferring deposits from the credit of one customer to the credit of another.

[1] In the overdraft system, as found in England, an overdraft is a right to use borrowing power; the loan is actually created when the borrower draws cheques under these overdraft rights.

Confidence and the Banker

The whole basis of all these banking operations rests on confidence on the part of the general public. This need for a basis of confidence can be seen at two levels. There is the confidence that some kinds of bank money can always be used for making any kind of payment within a country. In England, Bank of England notes can be used for settling any debt; this position has the force both of convention and of law. At the second level, there can be some kinds of bank money which need not necessarily be acceptable to all people in all situations, but which are still very widely acceptable and which can always be converted into the most generally acceptable form. In England, the bank deposit (transferred from person to person by drawing cheques) is in this category. Cheques are not acceptable in all situations; a restaurant proprietor or a shopkeeper who does not know me may insist on payment in cash (in Bank of England notes and coin). Nevertheless, cheques do have considerable advantages of convenience, so that in most advanced countries, a large part of money is held as bank deposits and transferred by means of cheques. Moreover, bank deposits are a convenient and safe way of holding money which is surplus to one's immediate needs. All the same, payment by transferring bank deposits is not always acceptable (or, for that matter, convenient); therefore, a depositor will always want to be quite sure that he can convert his deposit on demand into the most acceptable form of money (i.e. in England bank notes and coin). At this second level, therefore, there must be confidence in the power of the bank to pay cash on demand.

That such confidence is important is shown by past experience; there were many occasions in the nineteenth century in England and as recently as the nineteen thirties in the United States, when commercial banks were unable to pay out cash to all their depositors in a 'run on the bank' arising from loss of confidence. There are two main ways in which such a loss of confidence in a commercial bank can be avoided: the bank must run its affairs in such a way as to maintain the confidence of the public, and the government or some other public authority (usually the central bank) must ensure that the commercial banks never get into hopeless difficulties.

There are various rules which a prudent banker is well advised to follow if he is to avoid losing public confidence; for example, it is probably advisable not to mix up banking business with trading operations, because a trading loss is likely to lead to loss of confidence about the banking position. Of these rules, undoubtedly the most important is that a commercial banker should always possess sufficient reserves of cash to be able to pay out any likely withdrawals by his depositors. In addition, he should always possess sufficient reserves of assets which can easily and quickly be turned into cash without appreciable loss. This gives him a second line of reserves on which he can draw if his cash reserves are in danger of running out.

The need to maintain adequate reserves means that bankers are even more concerned with the form in which they hold their assets than are other transactors. They must always be careful to hold adequate reserves of liquid assets, which combine the attributes of convenience and certainty. Money held in the form of central bank notes and coin, available in each branch ready to pay out on demand to depositors, is clearly one example of such an asset. Another is a deposit held at the central bank; this can always be used very quickly to obtain further reserves of central bank notes and coin, to replenish the tills; it can also always be used immediately to settle debts to other banks.

In addition to these reserves which satisfy the needs for convenience and certainty as fully as is possible, the banker generally considers it worth while to hold certain assets which are not quite as convenient or as certain in value, but at the same time earn some interest. In other words, he may hold assets other than cash, which are not quite as liquid as cash, but are almost as liquid. He may, for example, be willing to make loans to other financial institutions which are repayable on demand or at very short notice. Again, a banker may be willing to hold part of his assets in the form of bills; he knows that he only has to wait a matter of months before any particular bill is repaid at its full value; moreover some of his holdings of bills can be expected to mature each week. Thus, bill-holdings provide a substantial degree of convenience and certainty (i.e. liquidity), while at the same time they earn an income.

While a banker must hold part of his assets in these liquid forms, he will not make much profit if he holds too many of them in liquid forms. For reasons outlined at the end of the previous chapter, interest rates on short-term securities are in general much lower than those on longer-term claims. Thus, a bank which is wishing to make a reasonably high level of profits can be expected to hold some longer-term claims, such as bonds. In most banking systems, banks hold substantial amounts of government bonds; in some countries they also hold appreciable quantities of bonds issued by private firms, despite the fact that such holdings are undoubtedly riskier—the advantage being that they generally earn more interest. In countries where English banking traditions have been powerful, such long period involvement in the affairs of particular firms has generally been regarded as too risky.

In all banking systems, however, banks are deeply involved in the financing of private firms, by making loans to them (and also to individuals). In principle, these loans are generally regarded as being repayable at quite short notice; in practice (even in England, where bankers have paid more attention to this need than in most other countries) it is frequently impossible for the bank to obtain repayment at all quickly, and many bank loans are of indefinite duration. Because of this and also because of the risks inherent in all loans to firms and households, the interest rates earned by banks on these kinds of loan are usually well above interest rates on bills and often above rates on bonds.

The perpetual conflict which the banker has to reconcile is that between making as big profits as possible, and maintaining sufficient assets in a liquid form to be able to pay his debts on demand. Only experience can show what is a suitable distribution of assets; and in acquiring that experience, earlier centuries (and in some countries, even this) have paid a heavy toll in the form of bank failures. Experience may be applied, either by self-restraint of the bankers themselves (as in England) or by the enforcement of minimum legal reserve ratios (as in the United States and many other countries). In England, it is considered that cash reserves should be equal to 8 per cent. of total deposit liabilities, and that reserves of liquid assets (including cash, loans at call and short notice to the discount market, and bills) should not normally fall below 30 per cent. of total deposit liabilities. The remaining 70 per cent. of assets are made up of holdings of government bonds and of advances (loans) to customers.

Control and Support of the Commercial Banks by the Monetary Authorities

By imposing minimum reserve requirements by legal sanction, the government or the central bank of a country can help ensure that the commercial banks never get into hopeless difficulties. But there are also more important ways in which the monetary authorities can ensure this. Of these, much the most important is the operation of the central bank as *the lender of last resort*. If the central bank is always, in the last analysis, willing to lend to the commercial banks, the latter need never get into hopeless difficulties. In most modern banking systems, therefore, the central bank is willing to provide assistance when the commercial banks ask for it.

All of this reflects a fundamental difference of aim between modern central banks and commercial banks. The main purpose of the commercial banks is to make profits for their shareholders; but the main purpose of central banks is not one of profit making. This applies both in the case of nationalized central banks and those where private ownership still survives. The most important purposes of central banks is to help control and stabilize the monetary and banking system. This they usually do in co-operation with the Treasury or finance ministry; the two taken together can conveniently be described as the monetary authorities. In this matter of monetary stabilization and control, which so closely concerns the government of all modern states, the central bank can never be completely autonomous and independent of the state—although most central banks still contrive to be much more independent of the government than any civil service department can be.

In carrying out their duty of acting as lender of last resort, central banks may impose stringent conditions; otherwise, the commercial banks could use the facilities provided by the central bank to obtain reserves sufficient to act as a safe foundation for as much lending as they liked. The central bank usually limits such actions by only being willing to assist the commercial banks by buying short-dated securities (bills) from the commercial banks (or alternatively only lending against such short-dated securities).

Moreover, such assistance is normally available only on terms which are unfavourable relatively to market rates of interest. The imposition of penal terms is

H

clearly a way to limit recourse to central bank assistance. It may be noted, however, that there have been important phases in history (e.g. the 'forties in both Britain and the United States) when the central bank has been willing to provide assistance to the commercial banks at market rates of interest. In these circumstances the commercial banks are under no pressure to limit their dependence on borrowing from the central bank.

But whatever may be the terms on which the central bank will give assistance, its actions have a powerful effect on interest rates, particularly on rates for bills, in which these transactions are usually carried out. Obviously, if the central bank is willing to lend at market rates, there is strong support for existing market rates; in fact, in the system of the 'forties in Britain and the United States, short-term interest rates were very stable (at very low levels). Again, if the central bank is only willing to lend at rates higher than market rates, this may well affect the level of market rates. For one thing, commercial banks will be unwilling to lend (by holding bills, etc.) at rates very far below the rate at which the central bank will lend to them, if they get into difficulties. Secondly, the commercial banks (and other financial institutions) are likely to increase the rates at which they themselves are willing to lend, if circumstances are such that they are being forced to borrow (or are likely to be forced to borrow) from the central bank. Here, then, lies the fundamental significance of Bank Rate in determining the level of short-term interest rates; Bank Rate is the rate at which the central bank will always lend in providing assistance to the banking system; short-term interest rates are never likely to move far below Bank Rate; they are likely to move up and down in step with Bank Rate, and they are likely to move nearer to Bank Rate, whenever the commercial banks are tending to become dependent on the central bank for assistance.

At this point, a second method by which the central bank can influence the monetary situation becomes relevant. It is now necessary to consider the significance of *open market operations* by the central bank. It is always possible for the central bank to buy or sell securities in the open market; these transactions may either be directly with the commercial banks or with the general public. These purchases or sales may involve either bills or bonds, at the central bank's discretion.

Transactions of this kind have two main kinds of effect; they may primarily be designed to have one or the other, but both will follow, to some extent, whatever may be the main purpose of the operations. One effect is that on interest rates; the other is on the size of total commercial bank deposits and therefore the total amount of money in circulation.

The first kind of effect, on interest rates, is the more obvious. In the first place, there is the very obvious and immediate effect that a sale of bills or bonds by the central bank tends to cause their prices to fall (interest rates to rise) just as would be the case if the securities had been sold by any other transactor. Similarly, a purchase of bills or bonds has the immediate effect of making the relevant interest rates fall. In the second place, there is an effect through the reserves of the commercial banks. To take the case of a sale of a security by the central bank to a member of the general public; payment for it will usually be made by means of a reduction in a commercial bank's deposit at the central bank. (The member of the public will pay by a cheque drawn on his account at a commercial bank payable to the central bank; when this cheque is settled by the commercial bank, the public's deposit at the commercial bank and the commercial bank's deposits at the central bank are reduced by the same amount.) The effect of all this is to reduce the ratio of the commercial bank's holding of deposits at the central bank to its total deposit liabilities. For example, if the original position of the commercial banks was the following:

Liabilities		*Assets*	
	£000		£000
Deposits of customers	1,000	Deposit at central bank	100
		Securities	500
		Advances	400

and the central bank then sold £10,000 of securities to the public, the immediate effect on the commercial bank's balance sheet would be the following:

Liabilities		*Assets*	
	£000		£000
Deposits of customers	990	Deposits at central bank	90
		Securities	500
		Advances	400

The ratio of deposits at the central bank to total liabilities has fallen from 10 per cent. to slightly over 9 per cent. If the commercial bank regarded the original 10 per cent. ratio as the minimum safe ratio, it can be expected to react rather quickly and to try to restore its original ratio. It can do this in several different ways, but whichever it uses is likely to lead to further rises in interest rates. It may, for example, appeal for assistance to the central bank, as lender of last resort; as we have already seen, additional reliance on the central bank is one reason why the rates at which commercial banks are willing to lend tend to rise. This is the way in which open market sales by the central bank can make Bank Rates effective: that is, to prevent market rates from diverging excessively from Bank Rate. By means of open market operations, market rates are driven up towards Bank Rate; such operations can always be used to force the commercial banks to follow changes in Bank Rate and change the rates at which they themselves lend. Another way in which the commercial banks may react to the decline in their reserves held at the central bank is to sell some of their security holdings; such sales of bills or bonds cause further upward pressure on interest rates. A third way in which the commercial banks may react is to reduce some of their lending; this they may do either by raising the interest rates at which they lend, or by refusing loans to some borrowers (bank credit rationing). In other words, they may make their loans dearer (dear money) or they may make them harder to get (tight money). In the latter case, the banks themselves do not raise interest rates. But it is very likely that some of the frustrated borrowers will switch to other sources of loans (e.g. hire purchase companies) at higher interest rates. Thus, in all cases, the secondary effects of open market sales by the central bank, arising from the decline of the commercial banks' deposits at the central bank, are likely to lead to further rises in interest rates.

The whole of the preceding analysis can be inverted for the case of open market purchases by the central bank; the effects are likely to be both immediate and secondary declines in interest rates.

The second kind of effect of open market operations by the central bank is that on the total amount of money in circulation in the country. The immediate effect of open market sales by the central bank to the general public is that the quantity of money in circulation falls by the amount of the sales; usually this fall will be a fall in the public's deposits at the commercial banks. In addition to this direct effect, there may well be secondary effects, resulting from attempts, of the kind already discussed, on the part of the commercial banks to restore their former reserve ratio. Thus, if the commercial banks restore their original ratio of deposits at the central bank to total liabilities by reducing loans (advances) to the general public, the quantity of bank deposits owned by the general public declines by the amount of the reduction in advances. Again, if the commercial banks restore their original ratio by selling some of their security holdings to the general public, the deposits owned by the general public also fall by the same amount. It is quite possible for open market operations to lead to greatly magnified effects on the total amount of money in circulation if the relevant ratio which the banks wish to maintain is small, and if it is maintained stable. Thus, if the commercial banks plan to hold stable the ratio of deposits at the central bank to total liabilities, the final situation in the numerical example already given will be something like the following:

After restoration of 10 per cent. reserve ratio

Liabilities		Assets	
	£000		£000
Deposits of customers	900	Deposits at central bank	90
		Securities (increased)	450
		Advances (reduced)	360
			———
			900

In order to restore a 10 per cent. ratio, a tenfold reduction in the level of deposits is needed.

In practice, there is an important limitation to the relevance of this analysis. In many countries, reserve ratios are not held at all constant; the decline to 9 per cent. might well have been tolerated as a normal fluctuation, so that no multiple reactions follow. But to the extent that the commercial banks maintain a constant reserve ratio, the analysis is relevant; open market operations by the central bank lead to a multiple reaction on the part of the total level of commercial bank deposits.

A further limitation on the usefulness of open market

operations by the central bank is that they can only be effective if there is an adequate market for bills or bonds in which it can operate. In many of the countries with less well-developed economic systems, neither of these kinds of market exists in more than a rudimentary form. In such countries, a remarkably simple substitute for open market operations is commonly used; this is the prescription by the central bank or the government of minimum reserve ratios, at different levels at different times. If, for example, the commercial banks have a 10 per cent. cash ratio and then the authorities say that in future they must work to a 12 per cent. cash ratio, then the commercial banks are driven either to borrow from the central bank or to sell securities or to reduce advances. In any case, there are the same kinds of effects on interest rates, on bank lending and on the total of money in circulation as follow open market sales. A disadvantage of this method is that it may be difficult to use for very small and frequent changes. On the other hand, this method has the great advantage that it can easily be used for very big changes; because of this, several countries with advanced financial systems (including the United States) make use both of variable prescribed ratios and of open market operations; the former are changed fairly rarely when big alterations in the situation are required; open market operations are used for smaller adjustments in the intervals.

Finally, it may be noted that instructions about reserve ratios are by no means the only instructions that may be given by the government and the central bank to the commercial banks. In the war and post-war years, direct instructions have been given to the commercial banks in most countries about the kind and amount of business they should do. It is hard to tell how effective such instructions have been; in many cases (including many of the post-war directives to the English commercial banks) there have been so many loopholes that the instructions have probably had little effect. On the other hand, there have undoubtedly been cases where such instructions have had big effects—for example the directive of the British Chancellor of the Exchequer in July 1955, setting a broad numerical limit to the amount of bank lending, and the post-war restrictions on consumer credit in the United States.

Chapter Eight

ENGLISH BANKING INSTITUTIONS

THE previous chapter was concerned with setting out the general principles of central and commercial banking. The purpose of this chapter and the next is to see how these principles have worked out in the particular case of England.

At the heart of the English banking system lies the Bank of England, which is the central bank. It has long carried out the basic functions of a central bank, by controlling the banking system and ensuring that the commercial banks maintain the confidence of their customers. Its relationships with the government have always been close—it has always been the government's own banker—and when the Bank was nationalized in 1946 the change was for the most part merely formal. The most important feature of the Act by which the Bank was nationalized is that it gave the Bank very considerable powers (which it did not previously possess) to give instructions to the rest of the banking system. In practice, these powers have not yet been used, because the Bank has a tradition of working through existing channels and by gentlemanly persuasion. Nevertheless, the existence of these powers is important, and means that if the Bank and the government so desired, heavy and possibly highly

unorthodox pressure could be imposed on the rest of
the banking system.

Because of the peculiar characteristic of banks'
liabilities—that they are used as money—and because
banks are particularly concerned with the kinds of
assets they hold, the most enlightening way of looking
at a bank's activities is to look at its balance sheet. In
the case of the Bank of England, this is about the only
way of getting much enlightenment—the Bank is very
reticent about discussing its policies (unlike most overseas central banks), but it is compelled by law to issue a
weekly balance sheet.

The Bank of England's Balance Sheet

The form of this balance sheet (of which that dated
28th February, 1958 is reproduced in the appendix)
is now a little anachronistic, having been laid down in
1844, in an attempt to establish an automatically
working system of control over the money supply. The
anachronism is that the balance sheet is split into two
parts, one being the balance sheet of the Issue Department and the other being that of the Banking
Department.

The balance sheet of the Issue Department is concerned with the issue of Bank of England notes—i.e.
ordinary ten shilling, pound and five pound notes. The
strict legal situation is that the Issue Department can
issue as many notes as it likes, if it holds gold to a
corresponding value. In addition, it can issue notes up
to a limit fixed by the government, which is known as
the "Fiduciary Issue". Since 1939, the Bank of England

has held practically no gold; almost all the country's gold reserves are owned by the Exchange Equalization Account, which is a government department. Consequently, the effective limit to the note circulation is the amount of the Fiduciary Issue. The government alters this limit from time to time, in accordance with the country's need for bank notes.

Most of the notes which have been issued are held by the commercial banks and the general public; but some are held by the Banking Department of the Bank of England, in preparation for increased demands for notes by the commercial banks and ultimately by the general public. These notes appear as an asset of the Banking Department and a liability of the Issue Department. If the split into two departments were abandoned, this item would drop out from both sides, and would be replaced by an item representing notes printed but not issued to the commercial banks and the public.

Apart from the very small quantity of gold, the Issue Department holds assets up to the amount of the Fiduciary Issue; it has bought these assets with the notes it has printed. Much the greater part of these assets is described as 'Other Government Securities'; these consist of bills and bonds which have been issued by the British Government. The first item on the assets side (Government Debt) dates back to the origin of the Bank of England in 1694, when it was granted certain banking privileges, in return for making a loan to the government of the day. The small item 'other securities' consists mainly of securities issued by

Commonwealth governments. The remaining asset ('coin other than gold coin') consists of copper and 'silver' coin bought from the Royal Mint and not yet put into circulation.

The first two items on the liabilities side of the Banking Department's balance sheet are not very important; the Bank's capital is now owned by the government; the item 'rest' consists of undistributed profits. The remaining liabilities are the deposits of people and organizations who bank with the Bank of England. Of these, the most important is the government, whose various accounts are included under 'public deposits'. In these, a special item ('H.M. Treasury Special Account') used to be distinguished; it was connected with United States military aid, and derived from the uniform rules imposed by the United States on all recipients of such aid. In the British context, it had little significance.

Although the transactions of the British Government are on a very large scale, its deposits at the Bank of England are not very big, and do not usually vary very much. For the most part, the government finds it more convenient to take up fluctuations from week to week and month to month in its payments and receipts by varying the amount of its short-term borrowing, done by issuing Treasury bills.

Much the greater part of the deposits held at the Bank of England are 'Other Deposits' (i.e. by depositors other than the British Government). Of these, the larger part consists of Bankers' Deposits—these are the deposits at the Bank of England of British banks whose main business is in the United Kingdom.

The remaining liability—'Other Accounts'—consists of deposits of overseas governments and banks and of the relatively small number of private individuals and ordinary industrial and commercial firms who still bank with the Bank of England. With minor exceptions, the Bank now does not open new accounts except for governments and banks, but it continues to run old accounts dating back to the days when it competed extensively with the commercial banks for ordinary banking business. It is now quite generally accepted that central banks should not compete for business with the commercial banks, since it is the central bank's duty to control the other banks and that would be difficult if they were also competitors.

The largest item on the assets side of the balance sheet consists of Government Securities—these are various kinds of British Government debt, which the Bank has acquired on its own initiative. The next group, called 'Other Securities: Discounts and Advances', consists of bills discounted for the Bank's customers, and advances made to them—in each case at the request of the customer concerned. A large part of this total comprises loans made to the 'discount market', at the market's initiative; the significance of these will be discussed at some length in the next chapter.

The other sub-category, 'Other Securities: Securities', consists of securities other than those of the British Government, which have been bought at the Bank's own initiative. Finally, the item 'Notes' has already been mentioned, and 'Coin' includes further 'silver' and copper coin bought from the Mint and not yet issued to the commercial banks and through them to the public.

The Balance Sheets of the English Commercial Banks

There are eleven important commercial banks whose main sphere of operations is England and Wales; all of them have hundreds, and some of them thousands, of branches. In addition, there are distinct (though generally closely connected) banks operating in Scotland and in Northern Ireland. Of the eleven English commercial banks, five are particularly large and have a close network of branches over the whole of England and Wales. These are Barclays, Lloyds, Midland, National Provincial, and Westminster; they are commonly known as the Big Five. The other six banks are concentrated in particular regions—for example, Williams Deacon's has a close network of branches in Lancashire and Yorkshire.

The eleven important English commercial banks are often referred to as the English Clearing Banks and as the Joint Stock Banks. The former title arises from the fact that they are the members of the London Clearing House. This organization clears cheques between different banks—as for example when a customer of Barclays has made a payment to a customer of Lloyds, the Clearing House passes the cheque through and keeps an account of the debt between the two banks which thereby arises for settlement. The second title—that of joint stock banks—arises from the fact that these banks are all joint stock companies (i.e. ordinary companies whose shareholders have only a limited liability); the title is historically significant, because in the nineteenth century many English banks were partnerships.

As with the Bank of England, the best way of getting an insight into the operations of the English commercial banks is by looking at their balance sheets; this can conveniently be done by analysing the combined balance sheet of the eleven Clearing Banks. This is summarized in the appendix.

It will be seen that on the liabilities side, there are two main kinds of item. The first, and smaller, is the item 'capital'; this represents the banks' liabilities to their shareholders. This kind of item is to be found in all company balance sheets and needs no special investigation. The other broad group of items on the liabilities side is of a kind peculiar to financial institutions, and is our main concern. It is called 'deposits', and consists of debts which the banks owe to their customers. These debts have arisen because a customer has paid notes or coin into his account at his bank, or because he has paid into his account a cheque which he has received from somebody else. In either case, the important thing about these debts of the bank is that a customer knows he can use them as money by writing a cheque, and also that he can transform these debts into other kinds of money (i.e. Bank of England notes).

Deposits of customers at English commercial banks are of two main kinds—deposits on current account, which are withdrawable on demand, and deposits on deposit account, where notice is required. These time deposits earn some interest for their owners, whereas demand deposits do not.

The assets side of the balance sheet of the commercial banks is rather more complicated. As has already been mentioned, bankers are more consciously concerned with the liquidity of their assets than most other transactors, simply because their whole business is concerned with the creation, purchase, and sale of claims. In the balance sheets of the English banks, there is a spectrum of assets; at the one end are the assets which have the least convenience and security of value; at the other end are the assets with the greatest convenience and security. In accordance with the principles discussed in Chapter 6, the general rule is that the least liquid assets earn the highest incomes, while the most liquid (cash) earn none at all.

English commercial banks have always tried to keep well clear of making loans which cannot be recovered for very long periods, or which are otherwise risky. We do not, therefore, find any highly illiquid assets in their balance sheets. The least liquid asset in the English balance sheets is called 'advances'; this consists of loans made to customers, usually given by granting them overdraft rights. When a customer is given the right to run up an overdraft, he can draw cheques and so make payments to other people (and obtain cash for payments not made by cheque) even though he has no deposit at the bank. There is, of course, always a limit to these overdraft rights, and banks only give their customers the right to run an overdraft if they are sure that the loan can be repaid. Generally speaking, this means that some security is demanded—for example, I may have to give the banker custody of shares or bonds which I own, so that he can sell them and recover his debt if I fail to repay. Strictly speaking, most bank advances are repayable on demand—but it is generally accepted that this is a legal fiction, and in fact many overdrafts continue to exist for year after year. Nevertheless, bankers do not like to feel that it would be difficult to get repayment at fairly short notice. For example, they do not like to make loans to a company against the security of machines or other fixed assets if a forced sale could only be made with difficulty. The ideal kind of bank loan has always been regarded as the loan to finance the holding of a stock of goods while they are being processed, or in the interval between their production and their sale—these loans have to bankers the virtue of being 'self-liquidating', since money is more or less automatically available for their repayment when the goods have been processed and sold.

Next to advances, in the spectrum of bank assets stretching from the least liquid to the most, comes the item 'investments'. This consists of bonds (for the most part issued by the British Government) which have been bought by the banks on the stock exchange. In the last decade or so, the tendency has been for the banks to concentrate on holding bonds with only a fairly small (perhaps five to eight) number of years to run to maturity. Nevertheless, the prices of these bonds can fluctuate quite sharply, as interest rates change, so that these assets are of somewhat uncertain value. At the same time, it is always possible to sell them, at whatever the market price happens to be, so that these assets are more convenient than advances, which cannot be transferred to anyone else. 'Investments', therefore, are relatively illiquid, but not as illiquid as advances.

Advances and investments together are often called the banks' 'earning assets', because they earn relatively high rates of interest; investments earn whatever happens to be the relevant medium- or long-term interest rate and advances earn a minimum of $4\frac{1}{2}$–5 per cent., and more if Bank Rate is high. Taken together, the value of these 'earning assets' was equal, on 31st December 1957, to 56·7 per cent. of the total deposit liabilities of the banks.

The remaining assets of the English commercial banks are often called the 'liquid assets'. Although the major part of these assets does earn some income for the banks, their main importance is that they are highly liquid—in other words, they can be used conveniently and without much risk of loss to help pay any debts which the bank has to settle. An important principle of English banking, which is now regarded by the Bank of England and the commercial banks as a fairly precise working rule, is that the value of these liquid assets should not be allowed to fall below 30 per cent. of a bank's deposit liabilities. It will be seen that on 31st December 1957 they accounted for 38·5 per cent. of total deposit liabilities. The significance of this rule will be seen in the next chapter, in the discussion of the Bank of England's control over the banking system.

There are three main groups of asset within the category of liquid assets—they are bills, loans to the discount market, and cash. Least liquid of the three are the banks' holdings of bills. A small part of these are commercial bills, which have been issued by ordinary commercial firms in connection with trading and manufacturing activities. Much the greater part, however, consists of Treasury bills, which are short-term debts issued by the government. The commercial banks do not hold brand new Treasury bills; they never hold Treasury bills which are less than a week old. Moreover, they generally prefer to hold Treasury bills which have run for several weeks, and so most of the bills they acquire are due to mature within a month or so. This means that the banks' bill holdings are highly liquid—it is only necessary to wait a few weeks, and the government pays up their full maturity value.

The commercial banks buy these bills from the *discount houses*—a group of specialized institutions which are often collectively described as the money market. There are twelve of these firms, and they are quite peculiar to the English system. Their importance lies in their intimate connexion with the methods by which the Bank of England controls the banking system. The discount houses make a business of buying, selling, and holding bills (including both Treasury bills and commercial bills); they provide a market in which the prices of these bills (and so some of the most important short-term interest rates), are determined, and they are the immediate providers of a large part of the loans made to institutions (in particular the government) which borrow by issuing bills. The discount houses get their name from one of the major elements in their business—that of 'discounting' bills. By this is meant simply buying bills which are not yet mature at a price below their redemption value.

The most important single way in which the discount houses influence interest rates on bills arises from the part they play in the weekly auction of new Treasury bills by the government. Each Friday, the government puts up to auction a declared total value of these bills; any institution can make offers (or, in market terminology, 'tender'), for minimum quantities of £50,000 redemption value. Among the bidders are overseas central banks, commercial banks with offices in London other than the English commercial banks,[1] and big industrial and commercial firms who have large sums of money on hand for which they have no immediate need. In addition, the discount houses make offers in this tender. In doing so, they act jointly, as a syndicate, offering a uniform price to the government in the auction. The government naturally makes the best bargain it can, and accepts the highest bids it can get. The situation that always arises[2]

[1] As has been noted earlier, the English commercial banks never hold brand new Treasury bills. They refrain from the tender by agreement, first reached in the mid-thirties, designed to prevent undue competition with the discount houses, which the commercial banks regard as institutions which should be preserved.

[2] 'Always' because the amount of 'outside', non-syndicate money available is never as much as the government wants to borrow.

is that the bids which are higher than those of the discount market syndicate never exhaust the whole supply of bills put up to auction; but these higher bids together with the whole of the syndicate's bids would more than exhaust the amount the government wishes to sell. The government therefore accepts the higher bids in full, and accepts a percentage of the syndicate's bid. No bids at prices lower than that of the syndicate are taken up. Thus, the result is that the syndicate's bid determines the maximum price at which the government can issue new Treasury bills—in other words, it determines the minimum level of interest rates on such new bills.

While the discount houses are the immediate providers of a large part of bill finance, their own resources are not sufficient for them to be able to finance more than a small part of the bills they hold. For the most part they act as capital intermediaries, and finance their holdings of bills by borrowing from the commercial banks. Apart from the relatively small item 'capital' (of shareholders, etc.), the liabilities of the discount houses consist wholly of 'loans and deposits'—in other words money borrowed by the discount houses. The predominant part of these loans comes from commercial banks (including both the English commercial banks and other commercial banks, Scottish, Commonwealth or foreign, with offices in London). On the other side of their balance sheets the greater part of the assets of the discount houses are Treasury and commercial bills. In addition they hold about a third of their assets in government bonds with less than five years to run to maturity—these holdings are less liquid than their bill holdings and so are riskier, but they earn more interest.

The loans which the discount houses receive from the commercial banks, and with which they finance their activities, are made for very short periods. Often, they are simply made overnight, though they are in fact frequently renewed. There is, therefore, a degree of risk in the activities of the discount houses—they take loans which are repayable at very short notice, and use them to finance the holdings of assets which are rather less liquid. Out of the interest rate differences corresponding to the different degrees of liquidity of their assets and liabilities, the discount houses make their profits.

The great attraction to the commercial banks of making loans to the discount market lies in the fact that they can be called in at very short notice—that they are very liquid. These assets of the commercial banks are the second of the three categories of liquid assets that were distinguished earlier, and whose importance can now be appreciated after our discussion of the discount market. They are described in the English banks' balance sheets as 'money at call and short notice'. The banks earn less on these loans than they would on Treasury bills, the difference being the profit the discount houses make out of the transaction. At the same time, these assets are very nearly as liquid as cash—a commercial bank can always acquire cash, simply by calling in a loan to the discount market or (more usually) failing to renew such a loan when it matures.

Finally, cash is the third and the most liquid of all

the assets held by the commercial banks. They hold it in two different forms, splitting their holdings about fifty-fifty between the two. One part is held as notes and coin in the tills and safes of the banks themselves; this part of the cash reserve is therefore immediately available for repaying the deposits of any of the banks' depositors (as when a customer cashes a cheque). The other part of the cash reserve is held as a deposit at the Bank of England (being part of the Bankers' Deposits in the balance sheet of the Banking Department). This part of the cash reserve is immediately available to individual commercial banks to settle any net payments it has to make to the other commercial banks, as when its customers have been making bigger payments to customers of the other commercial banks than have been made in the other direction. Moreover, deposits at the Bank of England can be used by the commercial banks to replenish their holdings of Bank of England notes and coin, if the need arises.

Since 1946, the agreed convention has been that the commercial banks hold cash reserves, either in their tills and safes or on deposit at the Bank of England, to an amount equal to 8 per cent. of their deposit liabilities. Before that time, the cash reserve percentage shown in the banks' balance sheets was 10 per cent. but it had long been generally known that this was not a genuine figure, but was based upon a process known as 'window-dressing', by which care was taken to have unusually large amounts of cash on the days on which balance sheets were published; the genuine average reserve was then about 8 per cent., and the convention accepted after the last war simply regularized the situation.

At one time, great emphasis was laid on the importance of the cash reserve ratio in the analysis of the English banking system. Recently it has been recognized that too much emphasis had been placed on it, and (as will be seen in the next chapter) the more significant convention nowadays is that liquid assets as a whole shall not fall below 30 per cent. of total deposit liabilities. The explanation of this is quite simple. If an individual English commercial bank finds, when it is making up its books at the end of the day, that its cash reserves are falling appreciably below the 8 per cent. ratio, it can immediately restore its ratio to the 8 per cent. level simply by failing to renew loans to, or recalling loans from, the discount market. Moreover, the other group of liquid assets held by the commercial banks (bills, mainly Treasury bills) are also maturing day by day at a fairly rapid rate, since the commercial banks for the most part hold bills that are near to maturity. If a bank fails to buy a new bill when an old one matures, it automatically builds up its cash reserves. Consequently, English banks are able to hold their cash reserve ratios much steadier than banks in most other countries.

This restoration of the cash ratio never involves the bank in any *penal* cost. The only cost the bank suffers is that it has to give up the interest it would otherwise have earned on the loans to the discount market or on the bills it might have bought. This means that all the items which a bank counts as its liquid assets can easily and quickly be turned into cash, without any penal cost being incurred by the bank. Although money at call and short notice and bills are not quite as liquid assets for each bank as cash, they are very nearly as liquid. The most important line of demarcation in the spectrum of assets is not that between cash and other assets, but that between the liquid assets as a whole and the earning assets. It is with the significance of this demarcation that we shall very largely be concerned in the discussion of the control of the banking system by the Bank of England, in the next chapter.

Chapter Nine

ENGLISH TECHNIQUES OF MONETARY CONTROL

THE main concern of a central bank, in controlling the monetary system of a country, will usually be with one of two purposes. It may be primarily concerned with influencing the amount of lending done by the commercial banks and with the amount of bank deposits held by the general public—in other words with the total size of the assets and liabilities of the commercial banks. Alternatively, the central bank may be concerned primarily with influencing the level of interest rates. In this case, it may either have a predominant concern with the level of long-term interest rates, or with short-term interest rates.

The important single clue to the understanding of the traditional methods by which the Bank of England has influenced the English monetary situation is that the traditional concern of the Bank of England has always been with influencing short-term interest rates. The effects of its actions on long-term interest rates and on the amount of lending done by the commercial banks has always been secondary: generally speaking, Bank of England action has not been designed directly to influence these magnitudes, and although it has always been accepted that there will be these secondary effects, their exact nature has rarely been carefully thought out by the authorities. This is something which has not been fully understood by economists until very recently, and has led to a good deal of misunderstanding about the British monetary system.

The explanation of the Bank of England's concern with the short-term interest rate has varied over time. In the old days of the gold standard, the main reason was that the most important influence on banking policy was the state of the country's gold reserve—and its ultimate connexion with the rate of interest will be considered at length in Chapter 15. In the thirties, after the gold standard had been abandoned, the main concern was to keep interest rates low, in order to help encourage investment and so reduce the level of unemployment. During the war, and in the years of the Labour Government, up to 1951, the policy of maintaining low interest rates was continued, even though inflation had become the main problem. Instead of using high interest rates to limit private spending it was decided to use non-monetary methods of controlling the economy; moreover, low short (and also long) interest rates were to the government's advantage at a time when it was piling up a great deal of debt, because this reduced the burden of interest charges on the budget.

With the arrival in power of a Conservative Government in 1951, the decision was taken to use monetary weapons once more to help control the economy. In the last few years, and particularly in 1955–7, considerable reliance has been placed on banking controls. The tendency of the authorities was for some time to continue to use something like the traditional methods, relying predominantly on effects arising from changes in short-term interest rates. It came to be realized, however, that the traditional techniques had limited success in achieving the results that were desired, of limiting inflation and improving the balance of payments.[1] As a result there has been a good deal of rethinking about the best way of operating monetary controls in present-day British conditions. A change in emphasis is now developing, away from placing the major emphasis of central banking policy on affecting short-term interest rates, towards attempts to use it to have more direct influence on the amount of lending done by the commercial banks and on the level of bank deposits.

The Bank of England and Short-term Interest Rates

The fact remains, however, that until very recently the primary emphasis has been on influencing short-term interest rates and that new techniques are still only in process of being thought out. The two main ways in which the Bank of England has done this have been through altering Bank Rate, and through purchases and sales of short-term securities at market prices. It will be convenient to cousider each of these methods in turn.

Bank Rate is simply the rate of interest (publicly announced each Thursday morning) at which the Bank of England is always willing to provide assistance to the commercial banking system, when that system wishes to increase its holdings of cash. ('The commercial

[1] See Chapter 10, below.

banking system' in this context includes not only the commercial banks themselves, but also the discount houses.)

The influence of Bank Rate on the commercial banking system is so close that some of the most important interest rates in the system are changed automatically with Bank Rate. The most familiar of these is the rate charged by commercial banks for advances to their customers; the rule is fairly generally accepted that the normal rate is $1\frac{1}{2}$ per cent. above Bank Rate subject to a minimum of $4\frac{1}{2}$–5 per cent. But the important question remains: why do short-term interest rates all move with Bank Rate? To answer this question, it is necessary to look at the significance to the banks of the rate at which assistance is always available to them.

The great peculiarity of the English banking system is that the tradition has long existed that the Bank of England normally channels this assistance through the discount market; the commercial banks themselves do not, as a matter of tradition, appeal directly to the Bank of England for assistance when their cash reserves are falling too low. We have already seen (in the previous chapter) that they have the simple recourse of calling in loans to the discount market, or of failing to renew those loans when they mature. What happens when all the commercial banks are calling in (or failing to renew) loans to the discount market is that the discount houses find themselves in difficulties. If they had no one to whom they could appeal for assistance this pressure might drive them bankrupt, because they might find it impossible to realize their assets quickly enough to repay their loans from the commercial banks. They would then be paying the penalty of having assets which are less liquid than their liabilities. But for nearly a century, the Bank of England has always been ready to provide unlimited assistance to the discount market, at a price. Thus, if the commercial banks call in loans to the discount houses, they always get repayment at once, because the discount houses can always appeal to the Bank.

Bank Rate, at which the Bank is always willing to provide this assistance to the commercial banking system, via the discount market, is a penal rate: its level always stands higher than market interest rates on high class bills (of which Treasury bills are now overwhelmingly the most important part). Thus, a discount house knows that it can always acquire cash to repay its debts, by selling bills to the Bank of England or borrowing from the Bank. But it also knows that it will suffer a loss on the transaction, because Bank Rate is higher than market rates. The discount houses therefore try to place as little reliance as possible on assistance from the Bank of England.

At the one extreme market rates for bills can never get higher than Bank Rate, because if they did, it would be in the interests of the discount houses to finance the purchase of an indefinite number of bills with the assistance of the Bank. At the other extreme, market rates will never fall far below Bank Rate, because the discount houses are very aware of the risk that they may be forced to appeal to the Bank for assistance, and they do not like to risk having to pay too big a penalty.

Consequently, the rates at which they are willing to lend (by buying bills) never fall too far below the rates at which they can resell the bills (if necessary) to the Bank of England. This means that there is very strong reason why market rates of interest on bills should follow changes in Bank Rate; as we saw in the previous chapter, the discount market tender always determines the rate at which the government issues bills. The tendency of market rates to follow changes in Bank Rate is reinforced by a convention of the English commercial banks that the minimum interest rate at which they will lend to the discount houses is 2 per cent. below Bank Rate. Since such borrowings from the English commercial banks are the major source of the discount houses' funds, they are never willing to lend (by buying bills) at rates less than 2 per cent. below Bank Rate; they must have a margin to cover their costs and allow for profits.

Thus, we see that Bank Rate has a close effect in determining interest rates on high quality bills—they cannot be outside the range whose upper limit is the current level of Bank Rate and whose lower limit is 2 per cent. below Bank Rate. For example, if Bank Rate is 5 per cent. the rate on Treasury bills will be between 3 per cent. and 5 per cent. Nor is this the end of the matter. The Bank of England can always change Bank Rate and so alter the limits of this range; by raising Bank Rate to 6 per cent. the range becomes 4–6 per cent. But in addition the Bank can strongly influence the exact position within this range of market rates. To consider how it can do this, we must turn to the second of the ways in which the Bank affects market rates—by itself buying or selling bills.

Part of the effect of Bank purchases or sales of bills on their price will be just the same as similar purchases by any other organization. Thus, by buying bills, the Bank tends to raise their market price and so lowers short-term interest rates, taking them further away from Bank Rate. By selling them, it tends to raise short-term interest rates, bringing them nearer to Bank Rate. Thus, the Bank can use these open market operations in bills to influence the level of short-term interest rates, within their possible range of fluctuation as determined by the level of Bank Rate.

On top of this are influences of a kind which only a central bank can bring to bear. If the Bank sells bills, whether to the general public or to the commercial banking system, payment for them is almost certainly made via the commercial banks, who run down their deposits at the Bank of England. This leads to a fall in their cash ratio, and they will act quickly to restore it by calling in loans they have made to the discount market. The discount market can only remain solvent in such circumstances by appealing to the Bank of England for assistance. Such assistance is always given—but at a penal rate. The discount houses therefore find they are borrowing from the Bank at a higher rate than they are receiving in interest on the money they are lending by holding bills. Obviously, the discount houses are inclined to withdraw from such an unprofitable situation, which they do by charging more for their loans—as by offering a lower price for Treasury

K

bills at the next tender. The effect of open market sales, therefore, is to force the discount market to borrow from the Bank and so to force the discount market to charge higher interest rates. By open market sales, the Bank can always force short-term interest rates up towards Bank Rate; it can always 'make Bank Rate effective'.

Up to this point, we have been concerned with operations by the Bank which move bill rates within the range of fluctuation imposed by itself. But it is possible for the Bank to have a much stronger influence than this on the precise level of market rates: if the Bank is ready to make unlimited purchases or sales at any price (i.e. any interest rate), then the level of interest rates on bills is precisely pegged at that rate. This is, in fact, what happened in the years of the Second World War and the post-war Labour Governments. The Bank of England was prepared to buy (or sell) as many Treasury bills as were offered to it (or demanded from it) at prices corresponding to a fixed level of interest rates on bills; in the early post-war years, this level was $\frac{1}{2}$ per cent. These operations were often known as 'back-door' operations, in contrast with the normal assistance at a penalty rate (Bank Rate) given at the discount office, or the 'front door', of the Bank. During these years the ordinary Bank Rate mechanism was still formally in operation, but it was never used. When the Bank would purchase unlimited quantities of bills at market prices, there was no reason at all why the discount market should pay a penal rate by using the normal facilities at Bank Rate.

Since 1951, the Bank has once again been unwilling to make unlimited purchases and sales at market rates—the back door is not necessarily open and the policy of low and stable short-term interest rates has been abandoned. The main purpose of this reversal to something like the traditional position has been the desire, in the inflationary periods of 1951-2 and 1955-8, to make money both dearer and scarcer, and so to limit spending by the banks' customers. The big question about making money dearer is whether changes in short-term interest rates of the kind normally experienced really have an appreciable effect on the desire of people to borrow. Probably they do not—such borrowing is typically used by firms to finance the holding of stocks of goods, and other influences (of the kind discussed in Chapter 5) are almost certainly far more important than interest-rate changes. There are, however, undoubtedly some effects that can be important: to the extent that changes in short-term interest rates lead to sympathetic changes in long-term rates, there will probably be quite substantial influences on plans for long-lived investment, such as the building of houses and roads.[1] These reactions are probably quite powerful, if long-term interest rates change substantially; at the same time, as we have seen, they are generally slow to come about.

The Bank of England and its Influence on the Willingness of Banks to Lend.

It is probable, therefore, that changes in short-term

[1] As explained above, p. 75.

interest rates which have been induced by the Bank of England have relatively little effect on the desire of the customers of the commercial banks to borrow. But this is by no means the end of the story. Central bank action can also influence the willingness of the commercial banks to lend; it can make money scarcer, by forcing them to ration credit and refuse loans to people who would normally be regarded as perfectly worthy borrowers. As has been argued in the preceding chapter, this can be done by using open market operations to influence the size of the liquid reserves held by the commercial banks.

It is very doubtful whether purposes such as these have played a big role in central banking policy in England until very recently. Certainly in the twenties, which was the last period before 1951 in which central banking control was used positively, the main concern was with short-term interest rates, and any effects on the banks' willingness to lend were regarded as by-products. It was commonly argued in the books of the period, as in the description of the British financial system in the official Macmillan Report of 1931, that Bank of England policy was designed to have multiple effects on bank lending, through the use of open market operations; but it is very doubtful whether this view is correct. The economists believed one thing and wrote about it; it is now reasonably clear that the bankers had no such thoughts in their minds. Their overwhelming concern was with the effects of short-term interest rates on gold flows in and out of the country—a matter to be discussed in Chapter 15.

What is more, the orthodox economists' view (as expressed in the Macmillan Report) was also rather misleading in another respect. The view was that if open market sales by the Bank of England led to a loss of cash reserves by the commercial banks, the latter would react by a tenfold reduction in their total assets (tenfold because the conventional cash ratio at that time was 10 per cent. rather than the 8 per cent. which became the rule in 1946). A simplified example of what was supposed to happen was given in the accounts in Chapter 7. Only in this way, it was argued, could the commercial banks restore their 10 per cent. cash ratio, which was (at that time) regarded as the minimum safe level.

What this argument ignored was the fact that, if any commercial bank found itself with less than the minimum cash ratio, it could restore the situation without undergoing any penalty, simply by calling in loans to the discount market (or by failing to buy new Treasury bills from the discount market when old ones mature). This forces the discount houses to borrow from the Bank of England and so pushes up short-term interest rates, as we have seen. But does it necessarily induce a contraction in the lending done by the commercial banks? In answering this question, two further questions have to be asked. One is whether the bills sold by the Bank of England were taken up by the English commercial banking system (i.e. the clearing banks *plus* the discount houses) or whether they were sold (directly or indirectly) to other holders, such as ordinary business firms or overseas banks holding balances in

London. The other question is whether or not the English commercial banks were initially holding more than the minimum of 30 per cent. of liquid assets—i.e. cash, plus money at call and short notice, plus bills. Only if the Bank sold some of the bills directly or indirectly to holders outside the English commercial banking system, and only if the English commercial banks are initially somewhere near the 30 per cent. limit, is there any reason why Bank of England sales of bills should lead to a multiple contraction of bank credit.

The first question is whether or not the bills move into the hands of some organization, other than the English commercial banks and the discount houses. It is, in fact, rather likely that the bills will have been taken up by the English commercial banks or the discount houses, who together hold a very large proportion of the total number of bills outstanding. If so, there is merely a shuffling around of liquid assets within the English banking system;[1] this influences short-term interest rates but does not influence the size of the total liquid reserves held by the banks. For example, if the Bank of England sells Treasury bills to the English commercial banks, what happens is that the banks pay by running down their balances at the Bank of England; they then immediately restore their cash ratio to 8 per cent. by calling in loans to the discount market. The banks now have a bigger proportion of their liquid assets in bills and a smaller proportion in

[1] Including the Bank of England, the commercial banks, and the discount houses.

loans to the discount market (money at call and short notice). This situation is quite satisfactory to the banks; they have been willing to take the bigger proportion of bills because the Bank of England has sold them on favourable terms, so that they earn rather high interest rates. The banks are therefore quite content; their cash ratio and their liquid assets ratio are both as they were before, so there is no need for them to take any further action.

What of the discount houses? They have had to repay money they had borrowed from the commercial banks. Normally, this compels them to appeal to the Bank of England for assistance, at penalty rates. And, as we have already seen, this tends to make the discount houses offer lower prices at the Treasury bill tender— in other words interest rates rise still more. The Bank of England can push all this process to the point where interest rates have risen as much as it desires; then, when they are high enough, it stops its sales of bills and everything settles down again. All that has happened is a rise in short-term interest rates but no reduction in the willingness of banks to lend.

But what happens if the bills get into hands other than those of the commercial banks and the discount market? The rise in interest rates on bills resulting from their sale by the Bank may make bills more attractive liquid assets to large industrial and commercial firms and overseas banks. In this case, we have to turn to the second question: whether or not the commercial banks were initially in a position where their liquid assets were near the 30 per cent. minimum ratio.

If the bills sold by the Bank of England are bought by an industrial firm or some other organization which banks with one of the English commercial banks, the transaction does lead to a loss of liquid assets by the commercial banks. The reason is simply that the industrial firm pays for the bills by drawing a cheque on its bank; this bank in turn settles with the Bank of England by drawing down its own deposit at the Bank. The commercial bank, in turn, restores its cash ratio at once, by calling in loans to the discount market, with all the further consequences discussed above. But the difference from the earlier situation is that the commercial bank itself has not acquired more bills to offset this reduced quantity of loans to the discount market. So in this case, the liquid assets ratio of the commercial banks falls: cash is maintained constant, bills are unchanged, but money at call and short notice is down.

At this point, the relevance of the second question is apparent. If the commercial banks were originally well above a 30 per cent. liquid assets ratio, the reduction in the ratio hardly matters and the banks need do nothing more. But if they were originally at that ratio, a decline is a serious matter—and the response is the classical one of a multiple cut in the other lending of the commercial banks: they reduce their holdings of securities and advances, by selling medium- and long-term government bonds and by withdrawing overdraft facilities.

The multiple cuts, even when they come, are rather small. In order to maintain a 30 per cent. ratio, the total reduction in the quantity of deposits has only to be three-and-a-third times as large as the originating loss of liquid assets.

The upshot of all this argument is that the effect of Bank of England operations in bills on the willingness of banks to lend is rather tenuous. There may well be no effects at all. What is more, even if there are any, the multiple reactions are relatively small—contrary to what used to be believed.

Funding

Because the effects of Bank of England operations in the short-term market on the level of bank lending are so small and so uncertain, and since changes in short-term interest rates do not seem to have much effect on the economic situation, the authorities switched the emphasis of monetary policy during 1955–6 towards other methods of control. These techniques were by no means new—but a realization of the inadequacies of the more traditional kind of open market operations led to a much greater tendency to rely on the technique known as 'funding'. By this is meant that the monetary authorities (including the Treasury and the Bank of England)[1] put fewer short-dated securities on to the market and more which are longer-dated; this technique reduces the monetary authorities' use of bill finance and increases the amount of their borrowing done by issuing bonds.

[1] So that the process can be brought about if the Bank sells bonds it holds and buys bills. Generally speaking, however, large-scale operations of this kind are most easily carried out if the government itself issues fewer bills and more bonds.

The difference between this technique and classical open market operations in bills is simple; in the case of funding, the monetary authorities are exchanging bills for long-dated securities, whereas in classical open market operations they exchange bills for cash. In each case, the authorities tighten credit by issuing more of a less liquid asset and correspondingly less of a more liquid asset (i.e. bonds rather than bills in the case of funding; bills rather than cash in the case of classical open market operations). But the important difference between the two, which explains the greater efficacy of funding, is that substantial amounts of Government bonds are held outside the commercial banking system, whereas only a rather limited number of Treasury bills is in the hands of non-bank holders. This means that funding is more likely to involve people and institutions other than the commercial banking system—and as we have seen in the analysis of open market operations, this is necessary if action by the Bank of England (and the rest of the monetary authorities) is to have multiple effects on commercial bank deposits, as opposed to mere effects on interest rates.

When funding is taking place, the authorities sell more long-term securities; a large part of these will be bought by individuals and institutions outside the commercial banking system and will normally be paid for by a reduction in the deposits of these individuals or institutions at the commercial banks. The commercial banks then settle with the authorities by reducing their balances at the Bank of England and restore their cash ratio by a reduction in their holdings of Treasury bills (or those of the discount houses, by calling in money market loans). The general public now has more bonds and less bank deposits; the commercial banks have less liquid assets (Treasury bills) and correspondingly less deposit liabilities. This means that the liquid asset ratio of the commercial banks is down; if it started near enough to the 30 per cent. minimum it falls so low that the commercial banks have to restrict their lending by selling medium- and long-term government securities or by cutting advances.

Funding is, therefore, likely to achieve multiple reductions in commercial bank lending, so long as the banks are initially sufficiently near the 30 per cent. minimum liquid assets ratio. But these effects are still relatively limited, with a multiplier of only three-and-a-third; and the price the monetary authorities have to pay is substantial and may appear undesirable. This price is a rise in medium- and long-term interest rates. Only if this happens—that is, if bond prices fall—can the general public be persuaded to buy more bonds from the monetary authorities. Moreover, when the commercial banks start reducing their lending, bond prices fall still more, to the extent that the banks sell some of their holdings of securities. The attractiveness of funding therefore depends largely on whether or not one considers a rise in long-term interest rates to be desirable. This may or may not be considered a good thing—one reason why it may not is that the government naturally dislikes having to pay relatively higher rates on precisely the kind of security of which it is coming to issue more. On the other hand, higher long-term rates may be considered desirable as a way of limiting private spending.

Other Techniques of Control

Because of some of the disadvantages both of traditional open market operations and of the funding technique, a number of other suggestions has been made regarding ways in which the authorities can act to restrict bank lending. One of the simplest is that the Bank should use the powers it already has (under the Bank of England Act, 1946) to issue instructions to the commercial banks about the way in which they hold part or the whole of their assets. After a good deal of hesitation, it was announced in July 1958 that, in future, the Bank of England might require that the commercial banks should make 'special deposits' at the Bank, which would not be considered as part of their liquid assets.

It remains to be seen how this new method of control will work out, when it is in fact used. But it does have clear advantages over the other methods which have been used to influence commercial bank lending. For one thing, it can always be used with ease to bring the banks' liquid assets ratio below 30 per cent. and so cause pressure on them—even if initially their ratio was well above 30 per cent. This contrasts with open market operations and funding, which have no effects on bank lending, unless they are carried out on a very large scale, if the liquid assets ratio is originally well above 30 per cent. Again, the new technique is attractive to the government, in comparison with funding, in that it does not compel the government to increase the proportion of borrowing at high interest rates for long periods, which happens if monetary stringency is brought about by funding.

It may be, therefore, that this new technique will sucessfully replace what was probably the most effective element in the use of monetary policy in the 1955–6 period—namely that direct instructions were given to the commercial banks by the government, telling them to restrict the level of their advances to their customers. Similar exhortation had been used with some success, at intervals throughout the post-war period; the instructions given in July 1955 were particularly successful, probably mainly because a clear limit was announced to the quantity of advances the banks could make. All the same, this rather arbitrary action was resented both by the banks and their customers.

We must, therefore, leave the discussion of the English monetary system in a rather unsatisfactory state—for the simple reason that the system has itself proved to be a much less satisfactory weapon of economic control than it was thought to be a few years ago. In a few years' time it will be possible to see whether the system will have more fully adapted itself to the time in which we live.

Chapter Ten

THE BALANCE OF PAYMENTS AND THE BALANCE OF TRADE

IT is now necessary to take account of economic relations between different countries. The three most important tools of international monetary economics are the foreign accounts of the countries with which we are concerned, and the concepts of the balance of trade and the balance of payments.

The foreign accounts attempt to record all transactions taking place between the residents of a country and foreigners in a given period. If all transactions are accurately recorded, these accounts must necessarily balance: this arises directly from the conventions of ordinary double-entry bookkeeping, in which each transaction is recorded twice. For example, if there is only one transaction between residents and foreigners in a given period, consisting of a purchase of £100 worth of goods from foreigners which is paid for with gold, the accounts will simply look like this:[1]

Receipts from Foreigners		*Payments to Foreigners*	
	£		£
Export of gold	100	Import of goods	100

[1] To the reader who finds it paradoxical to put an export of a receipt and an import as a payment, the best explanation as what is, ultimately, simply a convention is that the accountant sees a purchase of something as involving a payment and a sale of something as involving a receipt.

If, in addition to this transaction, there had been another, consisting of a loan by a foreigner to a resident of our country, settled in gold, the foreign accounts would be:

Receipts	£	Payments	£
Export of gold	100	Import of goods	100
Loan from foreigners	50	Import of gold	50

or more simply

Receipts		Payments	
Loan from foreigners	50	Import of goods	100
Net gold export	50		
	100		100

However complicated may have been the transactions that have taken place, the same rule applies: if all transactions are fully recorded, the foreign accounts (like any other accounts) must balance, simply because each transaction is recorded twice, once on each side of the accounts. But while this presentation is useful, particularly in giving an arithmetic check, it is not enough. The other fundamental tools of international monetary economics are the balance of trade and the balance of payments—and it is a perfectly familiar fact that these may often be in disequilibrium. In what senses, then, can we talk of there being balance of trade or balance of payments disequilibrium?

We can define trade or payments disequilibrium if we isolate certain elements in the foreign accounts for a past period, and then say that the situation was not in balance, if the remaining items on the receipts side are not equal to the remaining items on the payments side. There are two particularly useful ways in which we can isolate some items in the foreign accounts. One isolates all kinds of capital transaction from transactions consisting of the sale or purchase of currently-produced goods and services. The other isolates only certain kinds of capital transaction.

Capital Transactions and Income-creating Transactions

The distinction between capital account transactions and trade transactions[1] in international trade is precisely the same as that already drawn in Chapter 1, in our consideration of the economy of a single country, between transactions involving exchange of assets and transactions which create income. If a home resident sells goods or services to foreigners, the transaction creates income for him. Similarly, if a home resident spends some of his income on foreign goods or services, he creates income for the foreigner concerned. On the other hand, transactions by which home residents and foreigners buy claims from one another have no direct effects on incomes; an example of such a transaction arises when I subscribe to a foreign loan, thus acquiring a claim against foreigners.

If we record all the income-creating transactions between our country and foreigners, the difference between the amount earned from foreigners by selling goods and services to them and the amount paid to

---

[1] Often also described as 'current account' transactions.

them for the goods and services they sell to us is known as the balance of trade. For example, if we sell £100 million of goods in a year and £20 million of services (e.g. to tourists, shipping services, interest earned on loans), while they sell £150 million of goods to us and £10 million of services, the balance of trade is as follows:[1]

Receipts		*Payments*	
	£ million		£ million
Export of goods and services	120	Import of goods and services	160
Balance of trade deficit	40		
	——		——
	160		160

The balance of trade deficit is offset by an equal surplus on capital account (or of course a trade surplus by a capital account deficit). This arises directly from the fact that the foreign accounts as a whole must balance. The common sense of it is quite simple—to the extent that we have bought more goods and services from foreigners than we have sold to them, we must have transferred assets to them, or incurred liabilities to them.

These assets may be one of two main kinds, with

[1] This can be split into a 'visible' trade deficit of £150 million *minus* £100 million = £50 million and an 'invisible' trade surplus of £20 million *minus* £10 million = £10 million. Goods are 'visible' — they can be seen crossing frontiers and so are more easily measurable; beyon that fact, the distinction is not very important.

which we are already familiar. They may be short-term assets, such as gold (which is still widely used for international payments, although no longer within countries), bank deposits, and other short-term claims such as bills of exchange. The other main kind of asset is a long-term claim, such as a long-term loan or a share in a company. We can, for example, transfer long-term claims to foreigners by selling them bonds or by selling them shares in our companies.

There are many factors influencing such long-term capital transactions. To the extent that they are done by private individuals and organizations, the main determinants are the rate of interest or the rate of profit that can be earned in our country compared with what can be earned abroad, and the degree of risk attached to the investment—for example, the possibility of political troubles. In addition, many long-term loans are made by governments, usually for reasons which are predominantly political.

For our purposes, the most significant feature of this distinction between long-term and short-term inter-national capital transactions is that the former are usually 'autonomous' while the latter are usually 'accommodating'. By this is meant that long-term transactions are usually made for purposes of private gain or political advantage, independently of what is happening to other items in the foreign accounts. On the other hand, short-term transactions usually 'accommodate' themselves to what is happening to the other items in the foreign accounts. For example, if I buy foreign goods and pay for them by paying over a cheque to the foreigner, there is a flow of a short-term claim (in the form of a bank deposit) to the foreigner, which arises solely and simply because of the purchase of goods. Again, if I buy a bond from a foreigner it will be paid for by some method such as a switch of a bank deposit; here the flow of short-term claims accommodates itself to the autonomous long-term capital movement.

The Balance of Payments

As a general rule, a trader who acquires a bank deposit or some other short-term claim against another country will not want to hold it as such; and in fact he may not be allowed to do so, even if he wants to, if his country is short of foreign exchange. What generally happens, therefore, is that he pays it into a bank in exchange for a bank deposit expressed in his own currency. Ultimately, therefore, international settlements are usually made between banks. In most countries, the immediate day-to-day business is done by the commercial banks, but they in turn do not usually run up large amounts of short-term international claims or allow large short-term debts to foreigners to develop. Beyond the normal fluctuations of working balances, they generally pass on to the central bank any surplus of short-term international claims arising out of their day-to-day business and acquire from the central bank any excess of requirements over the amount being sold to them by their customers. In other words, the central bank is the ultimate source and holder of short-term international claims in most countries.

The international short-term claims of a country may be held by the central bank in the form of gold, of bank deposits in some other central bank, or in other foreign short-term claims such as Treasury bills. Likewise, a country's short-term liabilities will generally be owed by the central bank or the rest of the monetary authorities in forms such as bank deposits or Treasury bills.

The outstanding feature of these means of settlement is that they are all exhaustible. For example, if gold payments are the ultimate means of international settlement which a country uses, it is clear that, if the trade and long-term lending transactions with foreigners to which the flow of gold accommodates itself are persistently such that gold is flowing out to foreigners, a situation will eventually arise where the country has no gold reserves left. The same thing applies if payments are made by drawing on bank balances held abroad. And slightly less obviously, it is true if settlement is made by increasing the debts which our monetary authorities owe to foreigners; there is a limit to the amount of our money which overseas countries are willing to hold.

All this implies that the authorities must be deeply concerned with the net flow of short-term claims between our country and the rest of the world. If, on balance, we are losing short-term claims, there is a danger of exhaustion of our reserves, or of the willingness of other countries to keep adding to the balances they hold with us. Consequently, in defining the concept of the balance of payments, movements of short-term claims are isolated in the foreign accounts from movements of long-term claims and trade transactions. The example given earlier can be developed to show this. We can suppose that we received £30 million of long-term capital from abroad and lent £10 million abroad at long term. The foreign accounts can now be presented as follows:

Receipts		*Payments*	
	£ million		£ million
Exports of goods and services	120	Imports of goods and services	160
Long-term capital from foreigners	30	Long-term capital lent to foreigners	10
Balance of payments deficit	20		
	170		170

We have now simply isolated short-term capital movements from the other items in the foreign accounts. In total, our country has reduced its short-term claims against foreigners, plus its gold holdings, and increased its short-term debts to foreigners, by a total of £20 million. The amount of this net change in its short-term capital position is known as its balance of payments deficit for the period under consideration.

The relationship between the balance of trade and the balance of payments is simple. The balance of trade is said to 'improve' when exports of goods and services rise more than, or fall less than, imports of goods and services. When the reverse happens, the trade balance 'deteriorates'. The balance of payments is said to 'improve' when the balance of payments deficit gets smaller or the balance of payments surplus gets bigger. Again, in the reverse case, it 'deteriorates'. A balance of trade improvement will be accompanied by a balance of payments improvement, unless there is a counteracting change in long-term lending. If, for example, our country's exports rose to £135 million next year, while her imports were unchanged, her balance of trade improves by £15 million. If long-term lending is unchanged, the balance of payments also improves by £15 million, to a deficit of only £5 million. But if at the same time foreigners reduce long-term lending to us from £30 million to £10 million, the total effect is that the balance of payments deteriorates from a deficit of £20 million to a deficit of £25 million.

The other important point to notice is that there may be a balance of *trade* deficit and still a balance of *payments* surplus—or vice versa. In other words a trade deficit does not necessarily imply that a country is losing reserves, etc.; the difference is accounted for by long-term capital movements.

Chapter Eleven

THE BALANCE OF TRADE AND THE LEVEL OF INCOME AND ACTIVITY

THE balance of trade is intimately linked with two of our other major matters of concern—the level of income and activity, and the level of prices. Since these two are themselves closely interrelated, as we have already seen, the ideal solution would be to consider all three together. But to do that as a first stage is too complicated and it is necessary to split the problem into manageable parts. As a first step in the analysis of international monetary economics, therefore, it will be convenient to consider the relationships between the level of income and activity and the balance of trade. In this chapter we shall assume that all prices in the two countries remain constant throughout the changes under consideration; this might happen if both the countries with which we are concerned are industrialized and have substantial unemployment of men and machines, and if the exchange rate between the currencies of the two countries remains unchanged, so that the price at which one currency can be bought in terms of the other remains unchanged. In the next chapter we can consider some of the effects of price and exchange rate changes.

The conditions for an equilibrium in the level of

income and output are directly analogous to those already considered in the case of a closed economy. There can only be equilibrium if output plans and expenditure plans are consistent. The complications of which we have to take account when we allow for the existence of foreign trade are the following. One is that a part of income is spent on imports;[1] the other is that a part of output goes to exports. There are, therefore, three uses to which income may be put—consumption of home goods,[2] consumption of imports, and saving. By analogy with the concepts of the marginal propensity to consume and to save, we can now introduce the parallel concept of the marginal propensity to import; this is the proportion of an increase in income which will be spent on imports. By definition, the sum of the three marginal propensities—to save, to import and to consume home goods—is equal to one.

Turning to the output side, we find that there are now three uses to which output goes, and no longer two. In addition to consumption and investment,[3] a part of home output is absorbed by exports.

The representation of imports and exports in the national income accounts is quite simple. The national income accounts of the country whose foreign accounts

[1] And it will be assumed, for the sake of simplicity, that all imports are used for consumption. The analysis is fundamentally the same, but is a little more complicated, if we take account of the import content of investment and exports.

[2] And services. For the sake of brevity, 'goods' should be interpreted as including services in this and the following chapters.

[3] Which, we have assumed in footnote 1 above, has no import content.

we were considering in Chapter 10 might look like the following:[1]

Income		*Output*	
	£ million		£ million
Wages and salaries	900	Consumption goods	1,000
Incomes from property at home	500	Investment goods	280
		Exports of home-produced goods and services	120
		Value of output of goods and services produced	
Total income	1,400	at home	1,400

We can also add accounts representing the ways in which people spend their incomes:

[1] Another complication, which will be ignored here, is that the total amount of income received by the residents of a country is no longer equal to the value of the total output produced in the country. The main reasons are that a country's residents may receive income from property abroad, and that foreigners may own property in our country, from which they derive an income. If I own shares in a Malayan rubber plantation, I receive income (in the form of distributed profits) in England from output produced in Malaya. The effect of this is that Malayan output (domestic product) is greater than Malayan income and that British income is greater than British output. To generalize from this: a country's income is equal to the sum of the total value of its output (its domestic product) and the difference between the property income it receives from abroad and that it sends abroad (its net property income from abroad). This adds a new element to the income account; but the basic rule is still that although a country's income may not equal its output, output of a country's goods and services equals expenditure on its goods and services.

Expenditure

	£ million
Consumption	1,000
Imports	160
Saving	240
	1,400

It will be recalled that, in the case of the closed economy considered in Chapter 2, the fact that all output must go somewhere was reflected in the fact that realized investment always equalled realized saving, in the accounts for any past period. This identity arose directly out of the way we defined our terms; it was a shorter way of saying that, for the residents of a country as a whole, the part of total output not bought out of their current income must be equal to the excess of their incomes over the amount which they spend on the country's current output.

This rule still applies when foreign trade is taking place. But now there are two uses to which output can go, other than being bought from the current income of a country's residents. It can still go to home investment; but it can also go to exports. Similarly, there are now two uses to which the income of a country's residents can go, other than buying output of that country. The income can still go to saving; but now it can also go to buy imports. The consequence is that the shorthand version of the output-expenditure identity is no longer that investment must equal savings; it is now that

Investment *plus* Exports
must be equal to
Saving *plus* Imports.

This can be seen in the arithmetical example just given, on pages 161–2. £400 million of the country's current output is not bought out of the current income of the country's residents: £120 million is bought by foreigners and £280 million goes to investment at home. On the other side of the picture, total income of our country's residents is £1,400 million; their total expenditure on home-produced output is £1,000 million; the excess is £400 million, made up of £160 million imports and £240 million saving.

Still more simply, we can see that

Investment *plus* the Balance of Trade Surplus
must be equal to
Saving,

since the balance of trade surplus is equal to the excess of exports over imports.[1] Alternatively, we can say that the balance of trade surplus is necessarily equal to the excess of saving by home residents over home invest-ment. Perhaps the most commonsensical way of seeing this is that saving by home residents consists of the total additions to wealth owned by home residents. Invest-ment at home is the addition to the residents' holdings of real wealth at home. If additions to real wealth at home are less than total additions to wealth owned by home residents, then these residents must be owning

[1] Or the balance of trade deficit equals the excess of imports over exports.

additional wealth of some other kind. This consists of additional claims against foreigners (or additional real wealth abroad)—in other words, it is foreign investment. And as we have seen in Chapter 10, the balance of trade surplus is equal to the net additional claims against foreigners, i.e. to total foreign investment.

Conditions for an Equilibrium Level of Income and Activity

In exactly the same way as in a closed economy, a necessary condition for equilibrium in the level of income and activity is that output and expenditure *plans* must be consistent. We have seen that realized output and expenditure must be identical; but if plans were not consistent, then some of them will have failed to be realized. These failures lead to revision of plans; through such revisions, the economy moves towards a new equilibrium.

It follows from what has already been said that, for output and expenditure plans to be consistent, consumers' plans for saving and imports must be equal to businessmen's plans for investment, plus the plans of foreigners to import from us (i.e. our exports). If this is not so, some transactors will be disappointed, and a movement will take place towards a new equilibrium. The way in which this happens can best be seen by considering a disturbance to a pre-existing equilibrium, and following through the chain of events following the disturbance. As an example, we can see what happens after a change in the level of investment in one or the other country.

If a rise in plans for investment at home occurs when the situation was previously in equilibrium, the immediate effect is that already considered in the case of a closed economy. The increased expenditure by the firms who are carrying out the investment involves a rise in the level of household incomes, which leads to a rise in household expenditure. As far as the home country is concerned, a cumulative process of expansion in the level of output and income develops, which continues, for reasons already discussed in Chapter 3.

The new element in the situation is that a part of the increased expenditure by households involves increases in purchases of foreign-produced goods and services. Now, as far as the home country is concerned, this part of expenditure is a leakage from the expansionary process at home; if additional incomes are spent on foreign goods or services, they do not lead directly to increased incomes for other home residents, whereas that part of additional income which is spent on home-produced goods or services does lead directly to a further rise in output and so in incomes of home residents. As far as the direct consequences of a rise in expenditure are concerned, we therefore have two leakages: one part of a rise in home income goes into savings and, in addition, a part goes to imports. The amount which is passed on directly to income recipients at home is thereby so much the less, and the multiplier is correspondingly smaller.[1]

[1] These effects lead to an increase in the level of income which in equilibrium is $\frac{1}{s + m}$ times the size of the rise in the

What the leakage into imports does, however, is to provide an expansionary stimulus in the foreign country. Initially, there was no disturbance to the situation there, since we assumed the rise in investment plans to occur in the home country and that it involved no import content. But when rising income levels in the home country induced a rise in imports, the effects of the disturbance do spill over into the foreign country, in the form of an addition to total expenditure on goods and services produced there. In the usual way, this leads to an increase in output and income there.

Nor is this the end of the matter; the expansion in the foreign country involves an increase in *its* imports, and so leads back to a further increase in output and income in the home country. Thus, although the leakages into imports by the home country have no direct effect in increasing the level of output and income there, they do increase output and income at home indirectly, via the repercussions on the income of the foreign country.

Although the expansionary processes in the two countries reinforce one another, they nevertheless show a tendency to get weaker and weaker, and eventually to settle down to a new equilibrium. The reason is quite

level of investment expenditure (where s is the marginal propensity to save and m the marginal propensity to consume imports). Thus if $s = \frac{1}{10}$ (one-tenth of an increase in income is saved) and $m = \frac{2}{5}$ (two-fifths of an increase in income is spent on imports), then the multiplier is $\frac{1}{\frac{1}{10} + \frac{2}{5}} = 2$. In this case, only half ($1 - \frac{1}{10} - \frac{2}{5}$) of an increase in income goes to expenditure on home-produced goods and services.

simple: not all of the increased incomes in the two countries is spent on goods and services; some goes to saving. As income levels in the two countries rise, plans are made for more and more savings. This must eventually stop the expansion in the levels of income and activity in the two countries, as can be seen if for a moment we consider the world economy as a single unit and not as two separate countries. The only leakage from the circular flow of expenditure on goods and services in the world economy as a whole is the leakage into savings. When the level of savings in the world as a whole has risen by the same amount as the original disturbance in the form of a rise in investment in the home country, then equilibrium is re-established.

It is also possible to say something in general terms about the balance of trade between the two countries; this will be less favourable to the home country than it was before the disturbance, both during the process of adjustment to the new equilibrium and when that equilibrium is reached. Initially, when incomes and expenditure rise in the home country, its trade balance deteriorates as a result of the rise in imports. Subsequently, this leads to a rise in income in the foreign country and to a rise in its imports—but the reflection back is never complete if any part of the rise in foreign income goes to saving, as it can normally be expected to do.

Chapter Twelve

THE BALANCE OF TRADE AND THE TERMS OF TRADE

In the previous chapter we saw that the balance of trade is intimately associated with changes in the level of activity. Our concern will now be with the other major determinant of the balance of trade in a free market system; this is the level of prices of goods and services. In particular, it is necessary to consider the effects of changes in the prices of goods entering into international trade. Such changes can come about in either of two ways. Exchange rates may be altered; when sterling was devalued in 1949 from £1 = $4 to £1 = $2·80, British goods whose price remained unchanged in terms of sterling became cheaper in terms of dollars, while American goods became dearer in terms of sterling. The other way is simply that prices may change in terms of domestic currency. If sterling prices rise and the sterling-dollar exchange rate remains unchanged, then their prices can also be expected to rise in terms of dollars.

The *terms of trade* are a statistical measure of the relationship between the prices at which a country is able to obtain the goods it imports, and the prices at which it can sell the goods it exports. This measure is related to some base year; if export prices have increased 5 per cent. since that base year and import prices have remained constant, then the terms of trade are said to have 'improved' by 5 per cent. More generally, the terms of trade are an index of export prices divided by an index of import prices.

Although a rise in export prices in relation to import prices (or a fall in import prices in relation to export prices) is conventionally described as an 'improvement' in the terms of trade, it is important to note that this description only goes a part of the way towards describing whether such a change is in fact desirable for the country concerned. In some ways, an improvement in our country's terms of trade is a good thing and yet in other ways it may be undesirable.

In the first place an improvement in the terms of trade can be seen as a desirable change because it means that if our country continues to import and export exactly the same volume of goods and services as before the change, it will improve its balance of trade. And as we have seen in Chapter 10, this implies an improvement in its balance of payments, unless there happens to have been a simultaneous change in long-term lending. An improvement in the balance of payments is likely to be regarded as a good thing; it may mean that balance of payments difficulties are reduced or ended, or it may mean that the country can build up its reserves and so be in a stronger position to face any future drains.

Alternatively, the benefits of more favourable terms of trade can be seen in a still more commonsensical way. Just as an individual's real income is higher if the price at which he sells is high relatively to the price at which

M

he buys, so with a country as a whole. If a country's export prices are relatively high compared with its import prices, it can enjoy a higher standard of living in return for a given amount of work and effort, than if its export prices are relatively low, because it can get more imports in exchange for the same quantity of exports.

Unfortunately, of course, there is no advantage, either for an individual or a country, in selling at high prices if the effect is that so little is sold that it is impossible to buy all the things that you want from other people or from abroad. This possibility we have ignored, by assuming that the volume of trade is not affected by the relationship between import and export prices. It is, in fact, extremely unlikely that our country will continue to import and export exactly the same quantity of goods and services after a change in its terms of trade as it did before the change. For example, there are several reasons why its volume of exports is not likely to be maintained. One is that foreigners will be likely to be less inclined to buy our exports if they have become dearer; they will be inclined to switch towards buying their own goods, and the volume of exports is likely to decline. Another reason is that foreigners will have become poorer as a result of the change in the terms of trade; for example, if their export prices have declined this involves a direct reduction in foreigners' real incomes and so in their ability to buy our exports. A third reason is that any improvement in our country's balance of payments is necessarily a deterioration in some other country's; the loss of reserves that the other country may suffer may compel it to take action to reduce imports of our goods.

It can be seen, therefore, that an improvement in the terms of trade is not unequivocally desirable, because it may well involve a reduction in the volume of exports. Similarly, it may lead to an increase in the volume of imports, which again causes a tendency for the balance of payments to deteriorate. For example, higher incomes at home, because of higher export prices, may well lead to a bigger demand for imports. Again, if imports become cheaper relatively to home-produced goods, it is likely that some home demand will be switched from home-produced goods to imports. It is apparent, therefore, that it is inadequate to see the effects of changes in the terms of trade simply by looking at the improvement in the balances of trade and payments that would result, if the volume of imports and exports were to remain unchanged, simply because these volumes are most unlikely to remain unchanged.

It is therefore necessary to consider in more detail the relationship between the terms of trade and the balance of trade. It will be convenient to do this in terms of the dilemma that always faces a country. This arises from the fact that it is more pleasant to have relatively favourable *terms* of trade, but that if they are too 'favourable', exports will be so expensive and imports so cheap that the *balance* of trade will be relatively unfavourable; and if the balance of *trade* is too unfavourable, the balance of *payments* will also be unfavourable, and the foreign currency reserves will sooner or later be exhausted. The dilemma can therefore be summed up by saying that if the terms of trade are too 'favourable', the balance of payments will be unfavourable and the situation cannot be maintained. It may, therefore, be necessary to accept less favourable terms of trade in order to keep the balance of payments in balance.

Our analysis can conveniently start in a situation where a country is in balance of payments deficit and so is losing reserves. We will assume, for the sake of convenience, that this happens even though the balance of trade is in balance, because there is a steady outflow of long-term capital which the government wishes to leave unhampered (a situation not unlike several post-war years in Britain). Our problem is to ask what changes in the relationship between import and export prices (that is, in the terms of trade) will improve the balance of trade and so bring the balance of payments into equilibrium. As a stage in the argument, it will be assumed that the change in relative prices is to be brought about by an exchange rate change, and that all *internal* prices remain unchanged—for example, if sterling is devalued relatively to the dollar, all British goods become cheaper in America by the percentage of the devaluation and all American goods dearer in Britain by the percentage of the increased value of the dollar, but British goods in Britain and American goods in America remain unchanged in price. All this implies that Britain's terms of trade have deteriorated by the same percentage as the devaluation.

Exchange Rate Changes and the Balance of Trade

The important question that we have to ask is, how will the volume[1] of goods imported and exported respond to changes in the relative prices of imports and exports? The technical term which is a convenient measure of this degree of responsiveness to price changes is the *elasticity of demand*. If a 1 per cent. rise in the price of a commodity leads to a 1 per cent. fall in the volume demanded, the elasticity of demand is said to be 1; if a 1 per cent. rise leads to a $\frac{1}{2}$ per cent. fall in the volume demanded the elasticity of demand is $\frac{1}{2}$; if it leads to a 20 per cent. fall in the volume demanded it is 20, and so on.[2]

Now it is conceivable that the responsiveness of the volume of goods traded to the relative prices of imports may be very slight, or even non-existent. In that case, the situation is described by saying that each country's elasticity of demand for the other's goods is zero— demand is completely inelastic. This might arise if consumers in each country found imports had no possible substitutes. A change in the price of imports in either country, while the price of home-produced goods remains unchanged, then has no effect at all on the volume of imports demanded. Thus, we can consider what happens if Britain devalues sterling by 10 per cent. when both British and American demands for imports are completely inelastic. (In all these

---

[1] i.e. the number, weight or some similar physical measure
[2] If the elasticity is 1, the amount of money spent is unchanged; the price rise (fall) just offsets the fall (rise) in quantity bought.

examples, we shall assume for the sake of simplicity
that Britain and America are the only two countries
in the world.) Britain then buys the same volume
of dollar goods as before at an unchanged dollar cost;
at the same time, she sells exactly the same volume of
goods as before, at a price 10 per cent. lower in terms
of dollars. The net result is that her balance of trade,
expressed in terms of dollars, deteriorates by 10 per
cent. of the original value of her exports. Such a result
is unequivocally harmful to Britain; both her terms of
trade and her balance of trade (and so her balance of
payments) have deteriorated. To depreciate the exchange rate in these circumstances would clearly be an
inappropriate policy for Britain. In fact, the reverse
policy would be the sensible one to follow, since to
raise the value of the pound in terms of dollars would
improve the balances of trade and payments—and also
lead to an improvement in the terms of trade. In circumstances where the import demand elasticities of the
two countries are very low, there is no dilemma of
choice between relatively favourable terms of trade and
a relatively favourable balance of trade.

It is, however, probably rare for import demand
elasticities to be so low that an exchange appreciation
leads to an improvement in the balance of trade.
Usually, the responsiveness of import demand to
changes in import prices is quite substantial. In such
circumstances, an exchange rate depreciation (with its
accompanying terms of trade deterioration) is an
appropriate way of improving the balances of trade
and of payments. For example, to say that the British

elasticity of demand for American goods is 2 implies that a 10 per cent. rise in their sterling price, as a result of a 10 per cent. devaluation of sterling, will lead to a 20 per cent. fall in the volume demanded, so that the amount of *dollars* spent by Britain falls by 20 per cent. If the American elasticity of demand for imports from Britain is also 2, a 10 per cent. fall in their price to the American purchaser leads to a 20 per cent. increase in the volume demanded, and so to an approximate 10 per cent. increase in Britain's dollar earnings. On the side of both imports and exports, Britain improves her balance of trade. And it is also clear that total world (i.e. British plus American) demand for British goods has increased while total world demand for American goods has declined.

Obviously, there must be some intermediate point between the cases where the elasticities are so small that exchange depreciation leads to a deterioration of the balance of trade and the cases where it leads to an improvement. As an example of this situation, we can take the case where the British elasticity of demand for American goods is zero, and the American elasticity of demand for British goods equals one. Britain buys the same volume of dollar goods as before, at the same dollar price; dollar expenditure remains unchanged. British dollar receipts also remain unchanged; the American elasticity of demand for British goods is unity; this means that a 10 per cent. fall in their price in terms of dollars leads to a 10 per cent. rise in the volume bought, and American expenditure in terms of dollars is unchanged.

This example is a special case of a simple general rule. This states that, in the circumstances we are considering, a country's balance of trade will improve as a result of exchange depreciation, if the sum of the two countries' elasticities of demand for imports from the other exceeds one.[1]

Internal Price Changes

All this analysis of changes in the relationship between the prices of two countries' goods has been carried out in terms of an analysis of exchange rate changes. Exactly the same kind of analysis is relevant if such relative price changes are brought about in other ways. The most important other way is through a change in the internal prices of all (or practically all) goods produced in one or the other country. Thus, if America inflates prices by 10 per cent. while British prices remain constant, and the exchange rate remains unchanged, then the effect on the relative prices of imports and home-produced goods in each country is the same as that following a 10 per cent. exchange depreciation by Britain. Both in Britain and America, British goods are now 10 per cent. cheaper than they were relatively to American goods. So long as the demand elasticities sum to more than unity, the relative price change can be expected to lead to an improvement in Britain's balance of trade. At the same time, Britain's terms of trade have deteriorated by 10 per cent.; import prices have risen 10 per cent. and export prices are unchanged.

[1] In the example the British elasticity was 0; the American equalled 1; the sum was 1.

This analysis of the effects of a general price inflation in one or other country is highly relevant to the analysis of the effects of an exchange-rate depreciation. If, for example, Britain depreciates her exchange rate by 10 per cent. and then allows all prices (in terms of sterling) of goods produced in Britain to rise by 10 per cent., the whole effect of the depreciation is wiped out. The prices of all goods in terms of dollars are unchanged: American goods, because internal prices are constant there, and British goods, because the inflation of sterling prices cancels out the reductions in dollar prices of British goods created by the depreciation. Similarly, all prices in terms of sterling have risen 10 per cent.: American goods because of exchange rate changes, and British goods because of inflation.

In the final position, the terms of trade are the same as before the exchange rate change—but so is the balance of trade and payments, because the relationship between home and foreign prices is once again as it was, so that the volume of goods imported and exported will be once again as it was before the exchange depreciation.

This analysis is particularly relevant to the situation of a devaluation by a country which is more or less fully employed. In such circumstances, a general inflation of prices is very likely to occur after an exchange depreciation, unless the government takes active steps to prevent it. This can be seen by linking together parts of the analysis of this chapter and of the previous. If devaluation leads to an improvement in the balance of trade (as is probably the usual case) it thereby leads to a growth in total world expenditure on the goods of the devaluing country; the improvement in the balance of trade is an expansionary force in the same way as an increase in the level of investment. A new equilibrium in the level of income and activity is only possible when planned savings equal planned investment plus the trade balance—in the familiar way.

This is all very well in an economy which is not fully-employed; the expansion leads to a higher level of income and activity in the devaluing country and a lower level in the other country (because the devaluation caused its trade balance to deteriorate). But in a fully-employed economy, an expansion in the level of activity is impossible; so what happens is a rise in prices there, in the manner already analysed in our discussion of inflation in Chapter 4.

In addition, it is very likely that if there is full employment, a devaluation will lead to defensive reactions by transactors, and that these will aggravate the inflationary tendencies. Such reactions are likely, because (as we have seen) a devaluation, when all internal prices in each country are constant, leads to a deterioration in the terms of trade of the devaluing country, which implies a loss of real income for the residents of that country. Now, it is likely that they will try to resist this loss by attempts to maintain real income or real expenditure. To the extent that these defensive reactions are successful, inflation goes ahead. It is perfectly possible for all transactors fully to restore their pre-devaluation levels of real income and real expenditure, by pushing up prices by the same percentage as the devaluation—but if they do so, they cancel out all the external effects of the devaluation. It follows, therefore, that if a devaluation in a fully-employed economy is to have a permanent effect on the balance of payments, the government must prevent these tendencies to general price rises from wiping out the effects of the devaluation.

Chapter Thirteen

DIRECT CONTROLS OVER FOREIGN TRADE

WE have seen that if exchange rate changes are used to deal with a balance of payments deficit, it is usually necessary to accept the burden of a deterioration in the terms of trade. This burden may be considerable, especially if the elasticities of demand for imports of the two countries are relatively small (though greater than unity), so that a relatively large exchange depreciation is needed to bring about any given improvement in the balance of trade and payments. This may well be quite a common situation.

We also saw in the previous chapter that, if the prices of a country's exports are reduced relatively to the prices of its imports, more exports have to be sent out to buy any given volume of imports. This means that the balances of trade and payments can only improve after an exchange depreciation if the volume of imports is reduced and/or the volume of exports increased to an extent more than sufficient to offset this terms of trade loss. But if the reponsiveness of the two countries' import demands to price changes is relatively small (i.e. the demand elasticities add up to not much more than unity), then most of the effects of the relative price changes on the volumes of imports and exports of our country are swallowed up in counteracting the terms of trade loss, and little is left over to bring about an improvement in the balance of payments.

It is in circumstances such as these that it may be considered well worth while to use direct controls to deal with balance of payments difficulties. Such controls may be over trade or capital movements; as far as the direct effects on the balance of payments are concerned, the same advantage results if I am forbidden to buy foreign goods or services. Here, we shall be concerned with restrictions on trade in goods or services.

Direct controls may take various forms. The most usual are tariffs on imports and import quotas.[1] The latter are restrictions on the quantity or value of imports of various kinds that can be imported. Frequently, direct controls discriminate between different countries; for example, it is easier in Britain to get permission to import a German motor-car than an American; tariffs also frequently discriminate, by preference arrangements. The multiple currency systems to be found in many countries with rather inefficient administrative machines amount, in effect, to discriminatory controls: some currencies may be sold at particularly cheap prices (in relation to world market prices), thus encouraging importers to buy from countries accepting those currencies; or again, currencies for imports of certain kinds of goods may be sold at particularly high prices, in order to discourage those imports.

As a first stage, it will be convenient to discuss the

[1] Their effects differ considerably in many respects; here we shall be concerned with features they have in common.

effects of non-discriminatory controls, and to concentrate on one of the most usual forms, namely import controls. Then, subsequently, we can compare discriminatory and non-discriminatory controls.

The advantage of the use of controls, as a means of dealing with balance of payments difficulties, is that it is possible to use them to bring about an improvement in the balance of payments, without suffering any terms of trade deterioration. This clearly can be a big advantage if the alternative way of dealing with the balance of payments difficulties is to use exchange depreciation, and the demand elasticities are such that a relatively large terms of trade deterioration would be necessary. On the other hand, direct controls have other (and serious) disadvantages, which may frequently mean that it is unsuitable to use them.

It should also be noted that controls do not always avoid the terms of trade loss implicit in exchange depreciation. For example, a monopoly group of foreign exporters might increase the price at which they sell goods which become subject to import restriction, because the restriction on suppliers to the home market means that some home purchasers are likely to be willing to pay more for the limited supply available. If this happens, there has been a deterioration in the terms of trade as a result of the controls. Usually, however, it is possible to avoid most of these effects, even if there is a single foreign supplier; purchase by a monopoly home importer, rationing at home, and the use of import duties are all ways in which such difficulties can usually be avoided.

Assuming that the controls used are such that we can prevent the foreign supplier from increasing the price he receives, no terms of trade loss occurs. The prices paid for imports and received for exports are unaltered, so that by using controls to restrict the volume of imports, a country is able to improve its balance of trade and payments without suffering the terms of trade loss it would have to suffer if use were made of exchange depreciation.

This means that the total quantity of goods which residents of a country have to forgo, in order to deal with a balance of payments deficit, is smaller than when exchange depreciation is used. If import controls are used, a balance of payments deficit of £100 million is dealt with by a reduction in the amount of goods enjoyed by home residents of exactly £100 million. If exchange depreciation is used, some amount additional to this £100 million has to be given up, because the terms of trade worsen—each unit of imports has to be paid for with more exports than before.

There is another difference between the effects of import controls and devaluation, which may well work to the disadvantage of controls. When a country uses import controls to deal with balance of payments difficulties it forgoes the use of one kind of goods— namely imports. If, on the other hand, it uses exchange depreciation, it again partly forgoes the use of import goods, to the extent that higher import prices cause people to buy fewer imports; but in addition a part of the total amount of goods it forgoes is in the form of home-produced export goods. Foreigners buy more of our goods, and so a part of our home output, which we could enjoy ourselves if we did not have to deal with balance of payments difficulties, forms a part of the total amount of goods we have to forgo.

Now, it may not matter whether we deal with balance of payments difficulties solely by forgoing imports or partly by doing without imports and partly by sending out more exports. But, on the other hand, it may well be the case that a pound's worth of the goods which a country imports is more important to it than a pound's worth of the goods it exports. If this is so, the government may well think that it is worth while to give up more than a pound's worth of exports, rather than lose a pound's worth of imports.

This situation is likely to arise in practice if the decision facing a government is whether or not to impose additional import controls, when some are already in force. In such circumstances, it is likely that all the least essential and least important imports have already been choked off, and that if import controls are imposed, they will have to cut off imports of more important things, such as raw materials for industry. If in these circumstances the government chooses the alternative policy of exchange depreciation, the country has to give up more goods in order to bring about a given improvement in the balance of payments (because of the adverse terms of trade shift already considered); but some of the goods it gives up will be in the form of additional exports, because foreigners buy a bigger volume of our exports when they become cheaper to them. If the foreigners' demand elasticity is greater than unity, the volume of exports rises by a bigger percentage than the exchange depreciation, and there is a rise in the country's total earnings from exports (measured in terms of foreign currency). In that case, rises in the volume of exports after exchange depreciation make a net contribution to the solution of the country's balance of payments difficulties, despite the terms of trade loss associated with depreciation. This means that the contribution required from a reduction in the volume of imports in these circumstances is less if exchange depreciation is used than if import controls are used. This may be very significant, if imports are important enough to the country's economy; the terms of trade loss implicit in exchange depreciation may be acceptable, as a way of ensuring that the minimum possible reduction is made in the volume of imports.

The kind of consideration just outlined is likely to become more and more significant, the more stringently import controls are imposed, because the more this is done, the harder will it be to find imports that are not essential to the economy. Almost inevitably, therefore, it is likely that a point will come beyond which it does not seem worth while to deal with balance of payments difficulties by import restrictions; instead, it will seem better to use exchange depreciation, despite the terms of trade loss.

There may well be very powerful reasons why a country will not choose to make use of controls, even before this point is reached. One is that there is always a big risk that the use of these controls will provoke

N

retaliation by other countries. There is a certain risk of retaliation, whatever methods are used for dealing with balance of payments difficulties—devaluation has quite often been known to lead to retaliation in kind—but the dangers are particularly serious when direct controls over foreign trade are used. For example, the erection of tariffs by one country against the goods of another country is very likely to provoke retaliation in kind.

The end product of a tariff war (or other process of mutual retaliation in the use of controls) is quite likely to be less satisfactory for each country concerned than a system without any controls. The reason is simply that the barriers mean that each country produces at home goods which could be obtained at less cost abroad (or alternatively, that residents of each country are unable to buy abroad some things which they would like if they had free choice). The benefits of international division of labour are forgone, without even necessarily solving the balance of payments disequilibrium between the two countries.

Even if there is no retaliation, the imposition of direct controls over foreign trade reduces the extent to which advantage is taken of the international division of labour. But this loss may be considered worth while, to an individual country which does not push the use of such controls too far, and which does not suffer retaliation, for the reason that adjustment by methods involving full exploitation of the international division of labour (such as exchange depreciation) involve a terms of trade loss.

If the decision is made to use direct controls to deal with balance of payments difficulties, there may frequently be good grounds for imposing the controls in such a way that they discriminate between trade with different countries. The arguments are quite simple. For one thing, it is possible for a country to deal with retaliation more easily if discriminatory controls are used. For another, discriminatory controls commonly make it possible to maintain a higher level of world trade than if non-discriminatory controls are employed. If the volume of world trade is thereby held at a higher level, there is a strong likelihood that more advantage is being taken of the international division of labour.

It will be convenient to consider in turn these two advantages of discriminatory controls over non-discriminatory controls. Firstly, it is possible to deal with retaliation more easily, if discriminatory controls can be used. Thus, if country B imposes controls over imports from the whole of the rest of the world (consisting, we assume, of two other countries A and C), the immediate effect is to improve its balance of payments. But it may then happen that country C retaliates by imposing restrictions on all its imports; such retaliation may seem necessary to C, particularly if B's import restrictions have forced C into balance of payments deficit. At the same time, it may well be that A (the other country in the world) does not retaliate at all; this is particularly likely if the controls of B and C still leave A in a relatively strong balance of payments position. If this situation comes about it may be worth while for B and C to agree to reduce restrictions on the imports of one another's goods, while continuing (or even intensifying) restrictions on A's goods. In other words, discriminatory controls may be imposed by both B and C against imports from A. This, to a large extent, is what happened after the war; A can be taken to stand for America, B for Britain and C for the Continent of Europe. America was always in such a strong balance of payments position that she never retaliated when controls were imposed against her, and Britain and the Continent organized fairly liberal trade between themselves and firm restrictions on dollar imports. A complicated pattern of discrimination may be set up in a world of many countries, where countries who are willing to use controls do so in a way that discriminates most strongly against those countries who are least likely to retaliate and least strongly against those who are most able and willing to retaliate—and who are in a weak balance of payments position so that they are forced to retaliate. In practice, different countries have greatly varying power to influence the intensity of discrimination and the characteristics of the discriminatory system. In the post-war world, Britain has been in a particularly powerful position because of the importance of sterling as a world currency. If Britain refuses to convert sterling earned by other countries into dollars—if sterling is inconvertible into dollars—she can force many of them to discriminate against American goods. Hence the importance of the question of sterling convertibility, which will be considered at more length in Chapter 16.

It can be seen that in the kind of situation outlined

in the preceding paragraph, the volume of trade between B and C is maintained at higher levels if discriminatory controls are used than where use is made of non-discriminatory controls: discrimination means that B and C do not exclude one another's goods. This advantage of discriminatory controls can apply quite generally, and not merely to cases where retaliation is stronger from some countries than others. For example, we can compare the use of discriminatory and non-discriminatory controls as a means of solving the balance of payments difficulties both of country B and country C in our three-country world. The initial position can be shown by a table in which data about countries as importers are represented in columns and data about countries as exporters are represented by rows.

		Countries as Importers			Trade Balance
		A	B	C	
Countries	A	—	8	16	+12
as	B	8	—	8	− 8
Exporters	C	4	16	—	− 4
				Total Trade	=60

In this table, we see that country A, in the nature of things, exports nothing to itself, while it exports 8 to B and 16 to C. Similarly, A imports nothing from itself, 8 from B and 4 from C. Its total exports are therefore 24, its total imports 12 and its balance of trade surplus is +12. The problem is to solve the balance of payments difficulties of B and C; we can assume this is done if their balance of trade is brought to zero. Let us compare the effects of discriminatory and non-discriminatory controls imposed by B and C.

If B and C impose non-discriminatory controls, it is reasonable to assume that they will impinge with the same pressure on imports from A and imports from each other; if imports into B from A are reduced by 10 per cent., so are imports from C. If such controls are used, trade can be balanced in the following situation:

		Countries as Importers			Trade Balance
		A	B	C	
Countries	A	—	4	8	0
as	B	8	—	4	0
Exporters	C	4	8	—	0
				Total Trade	=36

In this situation, both B and C have halved their imports, both from A and from each other; on the other hand A's imports are unchanged (since A does not retaliate). Total world trade is quite drastically cut, from 60 to 36.

Now, if B and C are willing to use discriminatory controls on imports from A, the balance of trade deficit of each of them can be reduced to zero at much less cost in terms of the reduction of the total volume of world trade. A possible solution is the following:

		Countries as Importers			Trade Balance
		A	B	C	
Countries	A	—	0	12	0
as	B	8	—	8	0
Exporters	C	4	16	—	0
				Total Trade	=48

In this situation, B and C buy as much as before from one another, and solve their deficits solely by restricting imports from A. Judging by the criterion of keeping the reduction in the total volume of world trade to a minimum, this solution is much more satisfactory than the use of non-discriminatory controls; the higher the level of world trade, the more likely it is that advantage is being taken of the international division of labour. All the same, this criterion will not be the only one used in the actual process of bargaining which leads to the establishment of a discriminatory world trading system; for example, B might find it quite impossible to do without any imports from A (as is demanded by the last solution above).

Nevertheless, the examples given do point to a basic consideration. If use is made of discriminatory controls, it is possible to keep the volume of world trade (and more particularly, of trade by the countries originally in balance of payments difficulties) at higher levels than if non-discriminatory controls are used. At the same time, both discriminatory and non-discriminatory controls have the advantage that they can be used to avoid the terms of trade loss, which is nearly always implicit in using relative price shifts as a means of dealing with balance of payments difficulties. On the other hand, the arguments against making too much use of direct controls over foreign trade, which have already been outlined, apply to the use of discriminatory controls as well as non-discriminatory.

Chapter Fourteen

THE RECONCILIATION OF INTERNAL AND EXTERNAL EQUILIBRIUM

OUR concern in the remainder of this book will be with some of the more important mechanisms which governments can use to attain and maintain a position both of internal and of external economic equilibrium. One of the major concerns of all governments is with maintaining a reasonable degree both of internal and of external balance in the economy of their country. We have already seen in Chapter 5 what is meant by internal balance; it can reasonably be interpreted as full employment without inflation. In the long run, external balance is inescapable—a country cannot be indefinitely in balance of payments disequilibrium; sooner or later, something has to be done about it. This is particularly obvious in the case of a balance of payments deficit, because sooner or later this involves exhaustion of reserves. In the case of a balance of payments surplus, the only inexorable pressure is that the surplus must have as its counterpart the deficit of some other country, and its deficit cannot continue for ever. In addition, there is a strong reason why surplus countries should do something about their surplus, which is that by so doing they may reduce the strains of adjustment for deficit countries, and so make it easier to maintain international equilibrium.

It is useful to classify into four groups the main ways in which the government can influence a country's balance of payments. In the first place, it may be possible to change the flow of long-term capital. If the net long-term capital inflow increases, or the net outflow decreases, then (as has been seen in Chapter 10) a constant balance of trade involves an improvement in the balance of payments. In the second place, it can change the internal level of activity and output; as has been seen in Chapter 11, a fall in the level of activity almost invariably improves the balance of payments. Thirdly, it can change the relationship between the prices of domestically-produced goods and foreign goods. One way it can do this is by altering the exchange rate; another is to alter prices of domestically-produced goods (or keep them constant when foreigners' price levels are altering). As has been seen in Chapter 12, a fall in the price of domestically-produced goods relatively to foreign goods leads to an improvement in the balance of payments, so long as the two countries elasticities of demand for the products of the other are sufficiently large. Finally, various kinds of control can be imposed over foreign trade. Some of the effects of these have been considered in Chapter 13.

Many considerations will help determine which of the four methods of influencing the balance of payments will in fact be used in order to deal with a country's balance of payments disequilibrium. Undoubtedly, one of the strongest factors influencing the choice is the fact that any action taken to influence the balance of payments will also influence the internal level of activity in the country. (In just the same way as any action taken to change the level of activity will affect the balance of payments.)

Two of the methods of dealing with a balance of payments deficit are generally associated with internal expansionary forces and two are generally associated with internal contractionary forces. Usually, exchange rate depreciation and the tightening up of controls over foreign trade both lead to a tendency to internal expansion in the country using them; in each case, the action taken usually leads to a switch in demand towards goods produced in the country concerned. On the other hand, the other two ways of dealing with balance of payments difficulties are associated with contractionary forces at home. This is obvious in the case where a reduction in the overall level of expenditure within a country is used to deal with its balance of payments difficulties—the remedy itself is the internal contraction. The same kind of thing happens if a country uses an increase in long-term borrowing from foreigners or a reduction in long-term lending to them to deal with balance of payments difficulties. For example, if higher interest rates are used to attract increased loans from foreigners or to discourage loans to foreigners, they are likely to have some effect internally, by discouraging investment; this in turn tends to lower the level of activity.

These linkages between the internal situation and actions taken to maintain external balance are most important in helping to determine the correct policies to be used by governments wishing to restore or maintain internal and external economic equilibrium. Whether or not the policies being followed are correct depends largely on the initial situation in which the government finds itself when it decides to take action. Normally, one can expect that neither the internal nor the external situation will be in balance. For example, a country may find itself with too much unemployment internally and with a balance of payments deficit externally. Then it can do something towards remedying both the internal and the external disequilibrium by methods such as exchange rate depreciation or the imposition of import controls. As we have seen, these policies generally lead to internal expansion and to an improvement in the balance of payments. On the other hand, if it carries out simple internal expansionary policies, as by lowering interest rates or increasing the budget deficit, it tends to aggravate the balance of payments problem.

But if a country finds itself with a tendency to inflation internally and still with a balance of payments deficit externally, it can do something towards remedying both situations by reducing the level of total expenditure within the country—as by reducing the budget deficit or raising interest rates.

The first rule, therefore, is that governments should choose one of the right pair of remedies for the balance of payments situation. The appropriate policies can easily be seen in the table on p. 196.

To choose a simple policy measure, even if it is appropriate, is only a first step; it will move things in the right direction, but it will be a matter of pure chance if the use of a single remedy can lead to the full restoration of both internal and external balance. Thus, if a country with excessive unemployment and a balance of payments deficit deals with its problems by import controls of an intensity sufficient to deal with the external deficit, the internal effect will be expansionary.

Appropriate Policies for Dealing with Balance of Payments Disequilibrium

Initial situations	*Internal Inflation*	*Internal unemployment*
Balance of payments deficit	Internal contractionary policies (including higher interest rates)	Lower export prices (e.g. exchange depreciation or impose import controls
Balance of payments surplus	Higher export prices (e.g. exchange appreciation) or reduce import controls	Internal expansionary policies (including lower interest rates)

But it might be that this expansion would be inadequate to reduce the level of unemployment right down to the desired level; alternatively, it might be that the expansion would go so far as to push the economy over into inflation. It would only be by a very fortunate chance if the internal expansion went just far enough to bring about internal balance, and no further. Similarly, it would only be by lucky chance if internal deflation in an over-employed economy with a balance of payments deficit could precisely restore both internal and external balance; again, remedies of sufficient strength to put one situation right would generally undershoot or overshoot in dealing with the other situation.

Again, if it happened that the initial position was such that the internal situation was in balance but there was external imbalance, any kind of action taken to deal with the balance of payments situation would disturb the internal balance. Once again, a *single* remedy is inadequate to reach our *dual* aims.

Since a single instrument is not enough, the sensible thing is to try to use two remedies. For example, if an economy starts with unemployment and a balance of payments deficit and then the government imposes import controls sufficient to deal with the external deficit, unemployment will be reduced but might still be excessive. If so, it is reasonable to use internal expansionary methods (such as a budget deficit by the government) to do the extra amount necessary to bring the internal situation into balance. Of course, this internal expansion, taken alone, tends to push the economy back into external deficit, so that the import controls need to be a little stronger still to deal with the external situation.

This particular case is an example of the general rule that two instruments can be expected to be adequate to reach two aims of policy. This does not preclude the use of more than two; clearly it is no easy task to restore precise internal and external balance by a combination of two policies, if the restoration is to be done quickly and smoothly. The problem of establishing satisfactory international monetary mechanisms is basically the problem of devising methods by which this restoration can come about quickly enough and smoothly enough to avoid any exhaustion of a country's international currency reserves and at the same time to be politically tolerable.

Before the 1914-18 war, it was found possible to satisfy these aims adequately by a quasi-automatic mechanism—partly because much more unemployment was tolerable politically. In the inter-war period these automatic mechanisms proved to be quite unsatisfactory, and today it is realized that there must be a good deal of conscious direction of policy if the two aims are to be satisfied. All the same, the automatic mechanisms (such as those used in the gold standard) are still an important element in the more conscious and deliberate policies of the present day. It is therefore valuable to look at these mechanisms, not merely for historical reasons, but also as a basis for an understanding of the present position. This is what we shall be doing in the next chapter.

Chapter Fifteen

INTERNATIONAL MONETARY EXPERIENCE

1. THE FIRST FOUR DECADES OF THE TWENTIETH CENTURY

THE method of international adjustment that became established in the latter part of the nineteenth century and in the first three decades of the twentieth was the gold standard. The successful working of this system involved the acceptance of fairly long periods in which unemployment was relatively high; in the inter-war period, when international adjustment problems were bigger than before the First World War, and when the adjustment process worked less smoothly than before 1914, this price came to be regarded as politically intolerable, and the gold standard was abandoned in the nineteen-thirties, first (among the major trading countries) by Britain, then by the United States, and finally by France.

But in addition to the historical importance of the gold standard, all the important elements in that system have a relevance outside its immediate institutional limitations. In principle, the gold standard adjustment mechanism is one where exchange rates are fixed and where free market mechanisms are used to bring about adjustment to internal and external balance. The free market mechanisms include the effects (if any) of unemployment in reducing money wage rates, and the automatic banking effects of a balance of payments deficit; the latter might be reinforced by deliberate central bank action. Although the gold standard as such is very unlikely to be re-established, all these elements are an important part of the system of international adjustment which we find in the second half of the nineteen-fifties—to such an extent that some writers have spoken of the current system as the 'new gold standard'.

In the gold standard, exchange rates were almost precisely fixed by the monetary authorities of member countries, and direct controls were not regarded as an appropriate method of dealing with foreign payments difficulties. The heart of the adjustment process was through the direct relationship between changes in the level of activity and the external payments situation, and between changes in the level of activity and internal price levels, whose changes in turn affected the external payments situation. In the 'classical' gold standard, as it operated for some years before 1914, these effects were reinforced by the automatic operation of internal banking mechanisms in the participating countries; in the 'ideal' gold standard, which probably never existed in practice but which was once commonly believed to have existed, these automatic banking reactions would be deliberately reinforced by central bank action.

The technical manner in which fixed exchange rates were maintained between gold standard countries was quite simple. Central banks in participating countries would be willing to buy and sell gold in unlimited quantities at fixed prices in terms of their own currency; the difference between the buying and selling prices was very small, merely reflecting handling charges. (Frequently, these conditions were satisfied in a very simple manner—gold coins would circulate freely, and their face value was the same as the value of gold in them.) In addition, free import and export of gold was allowed. These conditions taken together meant that foreign currency was always available at prices which could not vary by more than the handling charges and the cost of shipping gold abroad; if I can always buy (or sell) an ounce of gold for £5 in Britain and sell (or buy) it for $25 in America, the sterling-dollar exchange rate can never move away more than fractionally from £1 = $5—if it were to move far, it would be profitable to buy gold from the central bank in one country and sell it to the central bank in the other.[1]

The problem we are concerned with is, how the gold standard mechanism led to a restoration of internal and external balance in member countries after some kind of disturbance to the situation. As a convenient example of a disturbance we can take the case of a change of tastes, which leads to a decline in total world demand for the goods produced by the home country, and a rise in total world demand for the goods produced abroad (which we can describe as the foreign 'country'). This disturbance involves a deterioration of the balance of payments of the home

---

[1] The limits to exchange rate variations, beyond which it is profitable to ship gold from one country to another, are known as the 'gold points'.

country and a contraction in the level of activity there, together with an improvement in the balance of payments and an expansion in the level of activity abroad.

The subsequent adjustment process arises from the effects of these changes on the level of activity. One element is a multiplier process similar to that discussed in Chapter 11. The initial disturbance leads to a multiple contraction in the level of activity in the home country and a multiple expansion abroad. The induced lower levels of activity at home and higher levels abroad in turn induce some improvement in the home country's balance of payments position. This multiplier element in the adjustment process therefore brings the balance of payments part of the way back towards equilibrium, but pushes the internal situation in each country still further away from equilibrium.

The second element in the adjustment process in the gold standard system is one whose operation can be very slow and uncertain. As a result of changes in the levels of activity in the two countries, changes may be induced in the levels of prices of goods produced within each country. In the home country, where the level of activity has fallen, the full gold standard adjustment process demands that money wages and prices should fall. Correspondingly, in the foreign country, the increase in the level of demand above the point of full employment leads to rises in money wages and prices.

This assumption of internal price flexibility in participating countries is essential to the full operation of the gold standard. As we have already seen, it is extremely doubtful whether price flexibility of this kind operates at all strongly in a downward direction in most modern industrial economies. In the nineteenth century and early twentieth century, there was perhaps rather more flexibility; unemployment did perhaps lead to rather faster falls in wages and prices than it does nowadays. By the late twenties, however, it came to be realized in Britain that there could be long periods of unemployment without causing significant falls in wages and prices. In 1925, Britain re-established the full gold standard, after the war and post-war disturbances, at the pre-war price of gold. It was realized that this tended to overvalue sterling a little, and so make British exports rather expensive in world markets, but it was thought that adjustment could come about quite quickly and smoothly, through the agency of declines in internal price levels within Britain. In fact, there was heavy unemployment right through the last half of the twenties, when the rest of the world was booming, but there was no really marked tendency for British prices to fall.

Of course, it is common for prices to rise if there are very low levels of unemployment, so the internal price adjustments of the gold standard mechanism could be wholly concentrated, in the form of inflation, in one of the countries (the foreign country in our example). In fact, however, the gold standard never did work this way.

There is, however, the important case where price flexibility comes about easily, and is in fact the normal rule. This is the case of primary-producing countries.

If it happened that the home country in our example was a primary-producing country, the normal effect of a fall in world demand for its products would be a fall in their price. This effect would arise immediately, and not indirectly through a fall in the level of employment and activity. No doubt one of the reasons why the system worked well before 1914 was that the most important adjustments taking place at that time did involve primary-producing countries; it was only after the First World War that the gold standard system had to deal with major problems of adjustment between industrial countries, such as those arising from the undervaluation of the franc, the overvaluation of sterling, and the German reparations problem.

It is now necessary to see how these internal price changes, which are the second fundamental element in the gold standard adjustment process, help lead to full restoration of internal and external balance in both countries, after there has been some disturbance. The mechanism is quite simple; it is that already discussed in Chapter 12. If the prices of goods produced at home fall, and if the prices of goods produced abroad rise, then the tendency will be for world demand to switch towards purchases of goods produced in the home country, and away from goods produced in the foreign country. These switches will be the bigger, the bigger are the demand elasticities for imports of residents of the two countries.

It is now necessary to consider how the two elements just discussed operate together to bring about full adjustment to internal and external balance. How the interaction operates in detail is a very complicated question to answer and cannot be considered here. Nevertheless, the broad principles are simple. Basically, the point is that the two elements provide the two methods of adjustment which we saw (in the previous chapter) to be necessary to bring about the two policy aims of internal and external balance.

As an example of the way in which the two elements work together, we can consider what happens when the stage is reached where the home country finds itself with an undesirably low level of activity and still with a balance of payments deficit, as a result of the operation of the first (multiplier) element; what happens as a result of the operation of the second (price change) element? Prices fall in the home country, tending to cause shifts in demand which raise the level of activity and improve the balance of payments; thus the relative price changes operate to correct both the internal and external situations from the position in which they are left by the operations of the multiplier element.

Three particularly significant points may be made about these operations of the gold standard mechanism. In the first place, full adjustment to internal and external balance demanded a period of excessive unemployment or inflation (as the case might be) in industrial countries involved. In the second place, the adjustment process could be extremely slow if prices were sticky in the countries between which adjustment was taking place. In fact in the twenties, it was so slow as to be almost non-existent. In the third place, the mechanism did not depend upon banking reactions, but on the operation of ordinary market forces in the markets for labour and for goods in each country. At the time when the gold standard was operating, it was normal to lay emphasis on banking mechanisms as the agency through which adjustment was achieved. A more accurate interpretation of the situation, however, is that the banking mechanisms were simply forces which could accelerate the adjustment substantially and could make it smoother. For these reasons it is worth our while to consider the banking mechanisms in the gold standard system. One of these mechanisms works automatically; the other depends on the discretion of the central bank.

If a country has a balance of payments deficit, in a system where balance of payments deficits are settled in gold, the commercial banks in this country will be buying gold from the central bank to make payments abroad on behalf of their customers.[1] These transactions reduce the deposits of the public at the commercial banks and of the commercial banks at the central banks by equal amounts. This means that the reserve ratios of the commercial banks fall. The effects are just like those arising from open market sales of securities by the central bank, considered in Chapter 7; here it is gold which is, in effect, being sold to the general public, instead of securities. And just as after open market sales, this generally leads to higher interest rates and a reduction in bank lending. These

[1] The precise mechanism is that the pressure of excess of demand for foreign exchange over the supply available causes a fractional rise in the price of foreign currency (perhaps by $\frac{1}{2}$ per cent.); this makes gold exports profitable.

in turn may cause contraction in the level of activity in our country, reinforcing the multiplier contraction which has already been considered. Correspondingly, these automatic banking reactions reinforce the multiplier expansion in the other country. Moreover, if the relationship between interest rates in the two countries alters, there will tend to be a flow of capital towards the country with higher rates, because it is a good place to lend and a bad place to borrow. This interest-induced flow of funds towards the country with a balance of payments deficit, where interest rates rise, counteracts and may reverse the flow of gold from the deficit country. These interest rate effects thus provide an alleviation to that country's gold position. This, then, is the automatic correction through banking mechanisms.

In addition, we must consider the deliberate banking reactions which would take place under the 'ideal' gold standard, if all countries were following what have been called[1] the 'rules of the game'. If these rules were followed, Bank Rate would be raised deliberately in the country losing gold and lowered in the country gaining it. These changes would reinforce the automatic effects on the level of activity and on international capital flows that we have already considered. There can be little doubt that Bank of England policies, both with regard to Bank Rate changes and open market operations, were, in the first three decades of the twentieth

[1] By the Macmillan Committee, which was largely concerned with explaining the unsatisfactory nature of the gold standard in Britain in the twenties.

century, quite predominantly determined by concern with the effects of changes in short-term interest rates on gold flows into and out of the country.

On the other hand, these 'rules of the game' were by no means invariably followed by other central banks. In fact, the French and American central banks often did precisely the reverse when the gold standard was restored after the First World War. Instead of taking action to reinforce the automatic effects of the gold standard mechanism, they frequently deliberately countered those effects, so that gold flows would not have any effects on the internal level of prices and activity. They did this by means of open market operations in securities—they would sell securities at the same time as they were buying the gold that the customers of the commercial banks were buying from foreigners. The automatic banking effects of gold flows would thereby be sterilized. The security sales in themselves were contractionary in their banking effects while the gold inflows were expansionary; the net effect was zero.

This process of sterilization was one symptom of the reasons why the gold standard was to fail in the stresses of the depression of the early thirties. For one thing, the subordination of considerations of internal balance to those of external balance no longer seemed as acceptable as it had done before 1914. For another, the adjustment process was perhaps slower than it had been, because trade unions resisted wage cuts more strongly. Finally, and most important, the strains and adjustments which the system had to deal with were much greater than they had been—strains such as the effects of war and post-war inflations, of generally disturbed post-war conditions, of German war reparation payments and of the rapid growth of American economic power. In addition, the strains were aggravated by the British return to gold when sterling prices were still rather high, and the French return at an undervalued parity. The gold standard failed because its automatic mechanisms were inadequate to bring about full adjustment of the balance of payments and the level of employment sufficiently quickly and smoothly.

The collapse of the gold standard marked the introduction of a period of experimentation in international monetary policy. To an important extent, the gold standard system had been based on absolute confidence in the immutability of existing exchange rates. But in 1931 Britain was forced to leave gold, and to allow sterling to depreciate; then in 1933 the United States left the old gold value of the dollar for no very pressing reason; after these two shocks the old state of absolute confidence in existing exchange rates could never be restored. In its place has come a world in which no one regards exchange rates as completely immutable, and in which an approximation to gold standard adjustment mechanisms is simply seen as one of several possible ways in which countries can adjust their economic situations to changes in circumstances. Gold is still (along with dollars and sterling) one of the main means of international settlement, but the full gold standard system as described earlier no longer exists, and is unlikely ever to return.

Flexible Exchange Rates

A significant element in the international adjustment process as it was operated in the nineteen-thirties (when there was serious unemployment in most manufacturing countries and when commodity prices were so low that there was widespread distress in the primary-producing countries), was the use of changes in exchange rates. The most important changes were those between the major trading currencies—the dollar, the pound, the French franc, and the German mark. The German mark was in a rather special position—its old gold value was maintained, at least formally, by rigid exchange and trade controls and a complicated bilateral trade and payments system. The other three countries each devalued in turn; Britain in 1931, the United States followed in 1933, and France managed to hang on until she was forced to devalue in turn in 1936. At the end of this cycle of devaluations, the price relationships between sterling, the dollar, and the franc were very much the same as they had been before 1931; each of them had devalued in relation to gold, so that the price of gold in terms of each of them was higher than in the late twenties. This meant that the value of the world's gold stock was much larger than it had been, which was one of the reasons why the problem of the insufficient supply of gold to maintain international liquidity, which had been serious in the late twenties, was no longer pressing. Subsequently, both the franc and the pound were devalued in relation to the dollar, largely because of the strains of the Munich period and the approach of war. The total effect was that it was only for about two years, from 1936 to 1938, that the pattern of the major exchange rates was the same as before 1931; this means that the exchange rate adjustments were a very important part of the international monetary history of the thirties.

While there was this series of adjustments in the exchange rates between the major trading currencies, the general tendency was for the other, less important, currencies to be attached to one or other of these three, by maintaining a constant exchange rate with this leader and following its fluctuations *vis-à-vis* other currencies. In this way there developed the systems of currency blocs, of which the first to develop was the sterling area. This included those countries which had close trading and financial ties with London, and followed the devaluation of sterling either in 1931 or shortly afterwards. All these countries were primary-producing countries, largely dependent on the British market; all of them held a large part (and generally most) of their international currency reserves in London. The hard core of the membership had political ties with Britain: these were the countries of the Commonwealth other than Canada and Newfoundland. In addition, the Scandinavian and Baltic states and a few other countries were members during the thirties.

The other two currency blocs were the dollar bloc and the gold bloc. The former simply consisted of the countries (mainly in Latin America) which pegged their exchange rates to the dollar, after 1933; this group largely consisted of primary-producing countries with close trading and financial ties with the United States. The gold bloc consisted of a few European countries (of which France was the leader) which hung on to the old gold parity until 1935-6, when they found their goods so seriously over-priced in world markets that they were having to carry an intolerable burden, in terms of internal unemployment, in order to maintain some degree of balance in their foreign payments.

The thirties were the most important period in which the world made use of flexible exchange rates as a way of bringing about international adjustment. In fact, full use was not made of this mechanism: for considerable periods of time the various exchange equalization accounts[1] operated to maintain exchange rates which the respective governments considered appropriate. Fully flexible exchange rates would react continuously to changes in market demand and supply of foreign currency; even the British Exchange Equalization Account was explicitly designed to resist speculative and seasonal pressures, and the American and French funds were intended to, and did, take up positions in face of longer-run commercial forces. Nevertheless, even though a world-wide system of fully flexible rates has never operated, it is valuable to see how it could operate—partly as an indicator of a situation towards which there was a strong tendency in the thirties, and partly because it has been suggested again

[1] Which were the official funds in each of the major trading countries which came at that time to replace the central bank as the official agency for buying and selling foreign currencies.

in the last few years that such a system would be desirable.

A flexible exchange-rate system can combine two advantages. Under it, adjustment depends very largely on the free play of market forces. But at the same time, this system avoids a major disadvantage of the gold standard system, with its fixed exchange rates—the disadvantage that the relationship between the price levels in two countries is altered by changes in the internal price level, induced by unemployment in the country with a balance of payments deficit, and by inflation in the country with balance of payments surplus.

This makes a great difference in the path of adjustment following a disturbance, such as the example of the switch in tastes we have already considered in looking at the gold standard case. In principle, there is no need under the flexible rate system for a spell of unemployment in one country or a spell of inflation in the other; for example, if there is a decline in world demand for the home country's goods, internal balance there can be restored quite quickly by expansionary internal policies, while the adjustment to external balance is carried out by appropriate exchange rate changes. By devaluing the home country's currency, its goods become cheaper abroad and foreign goods become dearer at home; this causes an improvement in the home country's balance of payments, as long as the elasticities of demand for imports of the two countries are large enough.

The characteristic feature of this adjustment process

is, therefore, that the internal situation in each country is to a large extent isolated from the external one, unlike the gold standard system, where the internal situation is subordinated to the external during the adjustment process. This difference is very important, especially where the avoidance of excessive unemployment is a dominant aim of policy, and where the gold standard adjustment is very slow in restoring internal balance; as an example, the gold standard adjustment process would have demanded intolerable increases in British unemployment in 1931. These kinds of consideration can be seen to be particularly important when it is remembered that the world never does settle down to an equilibrium; at best we are always in a process of adjustment to the disturbances which are always upsetting the economy.

There are, of course, limits to the extent to which the flexible exchange rate system can isolate the internal economy from external changes. The adjustment of the external situation depends on changes in the terms of trade, which move against the home country, so that it must, in some way or other, accept a decline in the real income that can be enjoyed in return for a given amount of work. Moreover, each action taken by the authority to influence the internal (or external) situation must inevitably have its repercussions on the external (or internal) situation. Thus, if expansionary internal action is taken, one of its effects will be to cause a deterioration in the balance of payments. Again, if the exchange depreciates and so causes an improvement in the balance of payments, there will be expansionary multiplier effects at home. Again, complete banking isolation is only possible if the effects of net purchases or sales of foreign currency by commercial banks from the central bank are very carefully offset—otherwise, as has been seen, a balance of payments deficit usually tends to rising interest rates and tighter credit. Smooth adjustment can only come about if the authorities carry out policies which pay careful attention to all these interactions.

While a system of flexible exchange rates has very real advantages, it also had disadvantages which have always meant that full reliance has hardly ever been placed on it. One of the most important disadvantages is that speculation about future exchange rates may be 'destabilizing'. If a country's exchange rate depreciates and this leads to expectations of still further deprecia- tions, people may decide that the currency concerned is not a good one to hold and that the country's goods will soon be cheaper still. If free market forces are operating on the exchange rate, such expectations may force it still lower. These risks are particularly serious in the case of a country owing a great deal of money abroad, which can easily be withdrawn—a speculative run on such a currency could be disastrous. This con- sideration is today undoubtedly one of the strongest arguments against a flexible exchange rate for sterling.

A second disadvantage that may arise from flexible exchange rates is that an additional element of uncer- tainty is introduced into international trade if traders do not know what exchange rates will be in a few days' or a few months' time. It can be argued that this uncertainty can seriously discourage international trade and so reduce the advantages that can be taken of the international division of labour. Whether the objections are really so serious is questionable; in most countries there are forward exchange markets, where traders can fix a price today at which they will buy or sell a foreign currency at some date in the future; but on the other hand, such guarantees are usually available only for a limited number of months ahead.

A third argument against flexible rates was common in the thirties; it was that exchange depreciation could be used as a beggar-my-neighbour remedy for unemployment; by depreciating, a country could switch world demand towards its goods and so increase activity in its industries at the expense of other countries. This argument was frequently used by Americans and was one of the reasons for the relatively rigid exchange rate structure intended by the Bretton Woods arrangements which were made during the Second World War and of which more will be said in the next chapter.

A fourth argument against a flexible rate is that the possibility of continuing exchange depreciation may remove one of the forces inhibiting governments from allowing steady inflation of the internal price level. The argument is that a government may take firmer action against internal inflation if the price of letting the inflation continue would eventually be the need to make a sharp reduction in the exchange rate; whereas if there is a flexible rate the effect of each bout of inflation is that the exchange rate slides down a little more. This argument may well be relevant to contemporary British conditions.

In practice, the disadvantages of flexible exchange rates have generally been regarded as being powerful enough to outweigh the advantages. All the same, it is hard to deny the basic advantage of adjustment through changing exchange rates, which is that external adjustment can be brought about with less internal disturbance than in a system with fixed exchange rates. Awareness of this consideration, together with experience of the disadvantages of flexible rates, had strong influence on the deliberations at the end of the war about the shape of post-war international monetary arrangements, which led to the establishment of the International Monetary Fund, which was intended to be the key institution in the new post-war system. Its successes and failures will be among our concerns in the next chapter.

P

Chapter Sixteen

INTERNATIONAL MONETARY
EXPERIENCE

2. THE POST-WAR WORLD

IN the last two years of the war, agreement was reached
between the Allies, notably between the United States
and Britain, about the framework of the world economic
system it was hoped to establish after the war. These
plans were strongly influenced by interwar experience;
in particular, the aim was to avoid heavy unemployment and the excessive use of controls over international
trade and payments.

The International Monetary Fund

The key institution in the new international monetary arrangements was to be the International Monetary
Fund, which operates in Washington as a Specialized
Agency of the United Nations. The Fund's Charter was
agreed in 1944; it was intended to set up a new system
of international monetary arrangements which would
combine some of the major virtues of the gold standard
mechanism and the flexible exchange rates mechanism
—it was an eclectic system. This was done by arranging that exchange rates should normally be held fixed
within narrow limits—but that they should be changed
when a country's foreign accounts were in 'fundamental
disequilibrium'. What such a situation of fundamental

disequilibrium would amount to was never closely defined—perhaps a precise definition is impossible. Still the lack of a definition has been a reason why it is not easy to identify when such a disequilibrium exists. Broadly, the term can be taken to mean a situation of persistent balance of payments disequilibrium which cannot be solved by maintaining or restoring internal balance either in the country concerned or elsewhere; alternatively, fundamental disequilibrium can be taken to exist if a country can only maintain equilibrium in its balance of payments by means of excessive unemployment or by imposing permanent controls over foreign trade and payments. The only acceptable solution to fundamental disequilibrium is, therefore, to change the country's exchange rates with other countries. This change would be a step change to a new level, which would be maintained thereafter. In general, it was intended that these changes should only be made after consultation with the Fund.

The intention was, therefore, to avoid the disadvantage of the gold standard system (in which exchange rates were fixed permanently) that equilibrium could only be brought about after a disturbance by means of a period of internal imbalance, which in the deficit country would take the form of unemployment. At the same time, it was hoped to avoid the uncertainties and the (possibly harmful) speculation involved when exchange rates were continually fluctuating, by providing that exchange rates would normally be stable; the step changes were generally expected to be unusual. In addition, the provisions for international consultation before rates were changed were intended to prevent the use of unnecessary depreciation, or the use of it in a manner causing unnecessary harm to other countries.

Basic to the way in which the I.M.F. system was intended to work was the need for each country to maintain internal balance, in the form of full employment without inflation. Since internal adjustments in prices and the level of activity were not to be used to deal with external imbalance, and since it was intended that exchange rate adjustments should only be used infrequently, it was necessary that provision should be made somewhere in the I.M.F. system for some means of absorbing the inevitable, though temporary, changes that must occur in a country's balance of payments. Foreign currency reserves are the standard method of absorbing such temporary changes, and also for allowing for the effects of more permanent balance of payments disequilibrium, before it is identified as being fundamental. If the I.M.F. system is to work successfully, all countries must hold substantial reserves of foreign currency; and one of the most important provisions of the I.M.F. arrangements was for an increase in the total reserves on which countries could draw, when they were in balance of payments difficulties. These provisions were made by the establishment of a sort of mutual aid fund to which each country made a contribution, partly in its own currency and partly in gold and dollars. Each country can, within limits, buy the currency of any other country from this fund, in exchange for its own currency; charges are made for this service until such time as the country resells to the

Fund the currency it has purchased; these charges become bigger, the longer the delay before the resale.

As a general rule, it was intended that the provisions for exchange rate changes, in cases of fundamental disequilibrium, and for Fund assistance in cases of temporary disequilibrium should, together, be adequate for countries to be able to maintain a sufficient degree of internal and external balance. But in addition, however, the I.M.F. system permitted a limited reliance on the use of controls to help maintain equilibrium. This was yet another element of eclecticism in a system which we have already seen to be an attempt to mix the best of the gold standard and the flexible exchange rate systems.

The I.M.F. Charter allowed three sets of circumstances in which controls could be used. In the first place, they could be used over payments for goods and services in the post-war transition period, which was intended to end in 1952. Secondly, controls could be used permanently over capital movements. In the event, it has proved very difficult to control all capital movements, even when there have been extensive controls over current transactions, and it is still less likely whether such controls can have much effect when there are no controls over current transactions—many capital movements can easily be disguised as current transactions.

The third set of circumstances in which controls can be used in the I.M.F. system has caused much more discussion than either of the other two, although it has never been invoked. This arises under the 'scarce currency' provisions, which may be used in two alternative sets of circumstance. In the first place, the Fund can observe what is called a *general* scarcity of a currency and can make recommendations about it; the post-war scarcity of dollars might seem to have been an admirable reason for using this clause. Secondly, there may be a *technical* scarcity of a currency, if the Fund finds it has sold so much of that currency to members that the Fund's holdings of the currency concerned are running out. If a currency is pronounced 'scarce' in this sense, other countries can impose discriminatory controls over payments to the country whose currency is scarce. In fact, dollars have never been technically scarce because so little use has been made of the Fund's resources in the post-war years; members of the Fund have made so few withdrawals from its holdings of dollars that they have never been in danger of exhaustion.

This failure of the Fund to come to grips with the dollar problem in the early post-war years led to a widespread belief that the whole I.M.F. system was stillborn. Undoubtedly some of its provisions will always remain ineffective—for example, it is very unlikely that there can ever be real international consultation when exchange rates are to be changed; leakages of information to speculators are all too likely.

In the first decade of the Fund's existence, the I.M.F. system was not in effective operation. The basic reason for this failure was that post-war difficulties proved to be much bigger and lasted much longer than was expected. The Fund's resources would have been quite inadequate to deal with the adjustments and the disturbances that have taken place in the post-war years, and (still more important) the governments of most countries were rather unwilling to rely on the adjustment processes envisaged in the Fund's Charter. The most important symptom of this unwillingness has been the post-war dollar problem and the widespread use of of discriminatory controls over trade and payments. From the end of the war up to the middle of the fifties, the problems of discrimination dominated the international monetary scene. In effect, it was decided that, even though the I.M.F. had not declared the dollar a scarce currency, nevertheless discriminatory controls were an essential weapon in the pursuit of a reasonable degree of international equilibrium.

Discrimination and the Dollar Problem

The most outstanding symptoms of the discriminatory system have been the existence of the dollar problem, and the importance of regional trading blocs, making use of their own internal payments systems, of which the post-war sterling area and the European Payments Union have been the most important. In addition, the system has been exemplified by the existence of many bilateral trade and payments agreements.

It may seem rather odd to describe the post-war dollar problem as a symptom of the existence of the discriminatory trade and payments system. The more usual way of looking at it is to say that discriminatory controls over payments to the dollar area were imposed as a consequence of the dollar shortage. As a way of looking at the surface of things, this is perfectly reasonable—many countries have discriminated against payments to those countries which only accept dollars, because the first group of countries finds itself shorter of dollars than of other means of international payment. Most countries found themselves relatively short of dollars in the post-war decade. They were unable (at current levels of prices, incomes, and exchange rates) to earn sufficient dollars to make dollar payments as freely as other payments. And since most countries were in this position, it was not generally possible for one country to make up for its shortage of dollars by converting into dollars other currencies of which it had adequate supplies.

This, however, is only the surface of the matter. The fact is that this situation has come about because some countries have, in effect, decided that discriminatory policies should be used to bring about international adjustment, rather than the more 'liberal' alternatives of changes in exchange rates and changes in internal levels of activity. Moreover, discriminatory controls were regarded as preferable to the alternative of using non-discriminatory controls.

In turn, this decision to make use of a discriminatory system was based on a view of objective conditions. For one thing, it was based on a view of the actions of other governments, and in particular on a belief (which has been justified) that the countries which have been discriminated against would not retaliate. Secondly, the decision was based on a view (which was probably correct) that any other method of bringing about international adjustment would be more burdensome than a policy of making extensive use of discriminatory controls. For one thing, non-discriminatory controls would probably have led to much bigger reductions in the volume of trade than discriminatory controls did. For another things it was not possible to rely solely on methods of international adjustment other than the use of controls. Long-term capital receipts and receipts of gifts (especially under the European Recovery Programme) helped alleviate the burdens of the situation very greatly, but were in themselves inadequate. Some considerable reliance was placed in the post-war years on exchange rate adjustment, the most important occasion being the extensive adjustments made at the time of the devaluation of sterling in 1949; there can be little doubt that these adjustments also contributed substantially to the solution of the post-war disequilibrium in the world pattern of payments. Reliance was also placed on restraints on internal spending, although again there can be little doubt that the world payments disequilibrium would have been much less serious in the post-war period if some countries had been more successful in checking their inflations.

In the event, however, it was considered impossible to place complete reliance on exchange rate changes and on restraining the internal level of activity; to have done so would have caused intolerable losses of real income to the inhabitants of the countries concerned. If full reliance had been placed on relative price changes it was expected, with good reason, that there would have been a sharp adverse movement in the terms of trade; undoubtedly, many countries' elasticities of demand for imports were very low at that time, so that a relatively big exchange depreciation would have been needed to bring about a relatively small improvement in the balance of payments. In fact, many people thought at the time that the demand elasticities were so low that an exchange depreciation would lead to a deterioration in the balance of trade of the depreciating country. If this view had been correct, it would have been a strong argument against any exchange depreciation, and might have been an argument for an exchange appreciation by the deficit countries. In reality, this view was probably unjustified; its main weakness was that it forgot the importance of substitution in third markets: for example, if Britain depreciated relatively to America, British manufactures would become much more competitive with American manufactures in Latin America, so that the depreciation might well improve Britain's overall balance of payments, even if conditions were so extreme that it had no effect at all on the quantity of goods traded directly between Britain and America.

The other way in which the deficit countries in the post-war world could conceivably have brought about equilibrium in their balance of payments would have been by holding back their internal activity so drastically that their foreign accounts would be in balance. Such a policy could hardly have been conceivable politically, and its purely economic effects might well have been disastrous, because the restraint would probably have had to be concentrated largely on industrial investment; if this had to be cut back, the future competitive power of these countries in world markets would have been so much the worse, because productivity increases are largely determined by the amount of industrial investment taking place.

In summary, then, it can be said that if the discriminatory system had been suddenly abandoned in the postwar decade, many countries would have been forced into serious balance of payments difficulties. In order to deal with these difficulties, it would have been necessary for them to adopt other policies, which they would have (most reasonably) regarded as being less desirable and less acceptable politically.

In the immediate post-war years, the disequilibrium in the world payments system was so acute, and the world's dependence on North American supplies of many essential goods was so complete, that adjustment by any system which did not use discriminatory controls would have been practically impossible. (This was pretty clearly indicated by the rapid and dramatic collapse, in the summer of 1947, of the attempt to re-establish a relatively 'liberal' system by re-establishing sterling convertibility.) Subsequently, the choice gradually became a real one; probably the discriminatory system could have been abandoned at any time after about 1948-9, without impossible cost, but undoubtedly at considerable cost. Since about 1952, steps have been taken to dismantle the system, and since about 1955, it has not been very important, although important relics of it still remain.

The hey-day of the discriminatory system was the period 1949-53. It was in this period that the sterling area and the European Payments Union were at the height of their importance as discriminatory trading and payments blocs. The sterling area had existed as such a grouping since the beginning of the Second World War; in Europe, there had been a lengthy period of confusion after 1945, marked by a complicated set of bilateral trade and payments agreements, which was eventually ended by the establishment of the European Payments Union in 1950. Both the sterling area and the E.P.U. system still survive as discriminatory blocs, but by now (1958) they are much less important as such than they were a few years ago.

The sterling area of the war and post-war years was a direct successor to the sterling area of the thirties—it continued, within narrower boundaries, the characteristics of being a group of countries with close trading, financial and political links with Britain, which held most of their reserves of international currency in London. On top of these continuing characteristics, which have now once again become dominant, a well-defined discriminatory trade and payments system was established, which was the most important feature of the sterling area in the forties and the first half of the fifties.

Very broadly, the position that developed with the war, and which was maintained afterwards, was that the sterling area was an area in which trade and capital movements were relatively free, while imports from outside the area and capital movements to places outside the area were subject to a good deal of restriction. In other words, the area was an important discriminatory grouping. The pattern of the discrimination has changed with time—at the most sharply defined stage, in about 1950-2, there was a three-tiered structure: sterling countries imposed strong discrimination against imports from the dollar countries (in particular the United States and Canada) and some discrimination against imports from other countries (of which the E.P.U. countries of western Europe were the most important). Since about 1952, the importance of discrimination has been steadily reduced. Today, the independent overseas members of the sterling area make little or no distinction in granting import licences between sterling and E.P.U. sources of supply and several of them make no distinction between sterling and dollar imports. And Britain now only discriminates to a very limited extent in favour of sterling area imports.

The result of these weakenings of the discriminatory sterling area system is that the area is coming more and more to be like the area of the thirties—to be a group of countries with close ties with London, which do their international banking there, and which also discriminate to a slight extent in favour of one another. There are, of course, great differences between the present situation and the thirties: the exchange rate between sterling and the dollar is now held constant within narrow limits; the membership of the area is smaller, is more precisely defined, and consultation between members is rather more highly organized. Moreover, in the thirties the liquid assets (the reserves of gold and dollars) and the quick liabilities (sterling balances) of Britain as banker to the area were about equal in size, so that a withdrawal of sterling balances could never break the bank; today, the quick liabilities are much bigger in total than our liquid assets.

Very broadly, the development of the European discriminatory trading system in the last few years has been like that of the sterling area. In the immediate post-war years, the European situation was very confused, with many bilateral agreements; by 1950 the situation had largely been stabilized and a smoothly-working discriminatory bloc was organized with the establishment in that year of the European Payments Union. The most important period of the life of the E.P.U. system was its first two or three years; since then, its importance as a discriminatory trading bloc has tended to decline, with the general movement towards a more 'liberal' trading system.

The membership of the E.P.U. is the same as that of the Organization for European Co-operation (a body set up in 1948 under the stimulus of the European Recovery Programme); it includes all European countries outside the Soviet bloc except Yugoslavia, Spain, and Finland. The fact that Britain is a member both of the E.P.U. and the sterling area provides an important link between these two systems.

The E.P.U. was intended to help prevent trade discrimination among European countries and to encourage the removal of restrictions over trade among members. Members agree not to discriminate between one another and to liberalize certain minimum proportions of their trade with one another. To help make these aims possible, the E.P.U. created additional international currency reserves, for use by member countries, so that there was a bigger cushion to absorb temporary fluctuations in the balance of payments between each member and the rest of the group taken as a whole. Each month, each member country reports its bilateral payments situation with every other member to the Bank for International Settlement; the sum of a country's surpluses and/or deficits with all the rest of the members is that country's 'accounting surplus' (or deficit). Each member settles this surplus or deficit with the Union; since all of a country's settlements with all the other member countries are finally balanced out in a single transaction, countries are under no pressure to treat payments to one member differently from payments to another (as they were when settlements were bilateral). For example, if Britain has a deficit with Germany and a surplus with France, she has an incentive under bilateral payments agreements to discriminate against Germany and in favour of France, by allowing French goods to enter more freely in order to use up the bilateral surplus with France. But under E.P.U. the surplus with France helps cover the deficit with Germany. The E.P.U. creates international currency within the area covered by the system (which for this purpose includes the whole sterling area); this is done by arranging that each country's settlements should be made only partly in gold or dollars; the rest is made by granting credit to the Union or receiving credit from the Union, as the case may be. These credit arrangements have varied substantially over the life of the Union. In its earlier days, the ratio between the part of the surplus or deficit settled by credit and the part settled in gold or dollars was on a sliding scale; more recently, settlements were fixed in 1954 at 50 per cent. gold or dollars and 50 per cent. credit, then in 1955 at 75 per cent. gold or dollars and only 25 per cent. credit. The effects both of the abandonment of the sliding scale and of the tightening up in 1955 were to make the settlement arrangements more like a system in which settlement is made purely in gold or dollars.

Corresponding to this reduction in the difference between the way of making payments to countries within the E.P.U. system and that of making payments to dollar countries, there has been a reduction in the importance of the E.P.U. system as a discriminatory trading arrangement. Dollar imports are now allowed into most west European countries much more freely than a few years ago, and in several (notably Germany, Holland, and Belgium) there is now no discrimination at all between goods from dollar sources and other imports.

Just as the existence of the dollar problem was based on a set of political decisions which in turn depended on a view of objective circumstances, so the decline in the importance of the dollar problem in recent years must be seen in the same terms.

On the side of objective circumstances, there are two main reasons why the burden of maintaining adjustment between the dollar area and the rest of the world is now much less heavy than a few years ago.

One is that European goods are much more competitive with American goods than they were a few years ago. In turn, this can be attributed to two main reasons. One is that production and productivity have been rising rapidly in all European countries, so that European goods are now in plentiful supply. The second main reason is that the prices of European goods are more competitive with American goods than a few years ago—partly as a result of productivity increases and consequent falls in production costs, but probably mainly because of the relative price changes brought about by the currency devaluations of 1949. Admittedly, a considerable part of the effect of those devaluations has been cancelled out by the more rapid inflation in many European countries than in the United States; nevertheless, there can be little doubt that the slow process of adjustment in trade pattern to the devaluations has been an important element in the adjustment of the first half of the fifties (an adjustment that was delayed by the economic disturbances associated with the war in Korea). All this has had the consequence that since about 1953 the United States has typically had a small balance of payments deficit with the rest of the world, which has meant that in most years the rest of the world has been able to build up its holdings of gold and dollars.

The other reason why the burden of maintaining adjustment between dollar and non-dollar countries now appears to be less heavy is that the American economy has been kept on a much more even keel than was generally thought likely a few years ago. One

Q

of the main reasons why it was often thought a permanent dollar problem was more or less inevitable was a belief in the inherent instability of the American economy. Moreover, it was thought that even quite a minor slump in the United States would lead to very heavy pressures on the balance of payments of the rest of the world, because American imports tend to fall off sharply in a slump. In the event, the American economy has been remarkably stable; none of the three depressions since 1945 (in 1949, 1954, and 1958) has got out of hand. Moreover, neither the recession of 1954 nor that of 1958 led to severe balance of payments pressures for the rest of the world taken as a whole, or for Europe in particular. Nevertheless, it is still very possible that quite a minor American recession could cause a great deal of harm to the balance of payments of the rest of the world; and it is quite certain that a major American recession would have disastrous effects on the balance of payments of other countries.

Largely as a result of these objective conditions, political decisions have been taken in the last few years which are having the effect of greatly reducing the intensity of the discriminatory system. These decisions have not only been based on these objective conditions —they have also been founded upon changes in views about the desirability of various possible policies in any given circumstances. Increased awareness of the disadvantages of controls and of the benefits of the international division of labour have made controls seem less attractive than they commonly seemed in the early post-war years.

Sterling Convertibility

The most fundamental political decision leading towards the abandonment of the discriminatory system was the British decision to move ahead towards the free convertibility of sterling into dollars. This decision is so important, partly because of the intrinsic importance of British trade and finance in the world, and partly because of the key position of Britain in the network of world trade and payments. The pattern of trade and payments is such that many countries traditionally used to obtain part of their dollar needs by buying them from London with their surplus sterling (London acquiring the necessary dollars largely through buying the surplus dollar earnings of the outer sterling area). To the extent that sterling convertibility has been re-established, therefore, countries have been able to buy all their dollar needs with sterling. A country enjoying convertibility rights feels itself under much reduced pressure to discriminate against dollar goods.

There were four main elements in the convertibility debate, which was at its height in 1952-3. The first was simply the question whether convertibility was desirable, or whether (on the other hand) the attempt should be made to maintain a permanent discriminatory system. Here, the decision went clearly in favour of the pro-convertibility school. The second element concerned the speed with which the movement should be made—should it be slow, or should it be done quickly and sharply? Here the decision went to the cautious school—in the last few years there has been a slow and undramatic movement towards convertibility and a 'liberal' system.

The third decision was one of priority: should convertibility be given first to residents of sterling area countries (by relaxing the exchange controls imposed on each of them over payments to the dollar area) or should it be given first to other countries? Here there has been no clear victory for either school. As we have seen, restrictions on dollar spending in sterling countries are much less strong than they were a few years ago. At the same time, there is now very nearly full convertibility for residents of non-sterling countries. The most important part of the sterling bank balances held by residents of non-sterling area countries (including banks in those countries) is known as transferable sterling. This money can be used freely to make payments to all countries outside the dollar area —it is one of the means used to maintain London's position as an international banking centre. Up to 1954, the British authorities made some attempt to prevent the purchase or sale of transferable sterling against dollars; in fact, such transactions always did take place, usually with sterling much cheaper in relation to dollars than was indicated by the official exchange rate of approximately $2·80—the reason being that sterling was a less attractive currency to use than dollars (because it could not buy American goods) or to hold (because most people thought, most of the time, that sterling depreciation was more likely than appreciation). In 1954, the British authorities gave up their attempts to prevent these transactions between transferable sterling and dollars. Then in 1955, the British authorities announced that in future they would be prepared to operate in the markets (which are mainly in Zurich and New York) where these transactions take place. Since then, they have not allowed the rate at which dollars can be bought with transferable sterling to fall more than $1-1\frac{1}{2}$ per cent. below the official rate. In other words, the British authorities are willing to convert sterling into dollars for people living outside the sterling area, at the price of a surcharge of $1-1\frac{1}{2}$ per cent. Most holders of sterling who would prefer dollars are not likely to be discouraged by such a small surcharge—for them sterling is effectively convertible. On the other hand, other holders are discouraged, and to that extent, convertibility is, at the time of writing (1958), not fully established. It is clear, however, that we are very near to it.

The fourth, and last, question in the convertibility discussion is still not fully answered. This is the question of the international monetary adjustment method to be used after the abandonment of the discriminatory system. For example, some people have argued that internal and external balance can only be maintained if exchange rates are allowed to fluctuate, while others consider that the disadvantages of flexible exchange rates greatly outweigh their advantages.

The Current Position

The only thing that can be said with confidence about the current position is that it is widely realized that we can place only limited reliance on purely automatic systems of adjustment, such as the gold standard or a purely flexible exchange rate system, and that any satisfactory adjustment process needs a good deal of conscious planning. Very broadly, the trend of movement since about 1954 has been towards a system rather like that planned at the end of the war. As in the proposed I.M.F. system, individual countries have tried to maintain internal balance, controls have been used as little as possible, and there has been a great reluctance to use exchange rate changes.

This reluctance has been so great that some writers have seen the present-day system as a new gold standard. As things have worked out, there is a very important, though still somewhat limited, element of truth in this. In the last few years, the countries with serious balance of payments deficits have also, for the most part, been countries with more internal inflation than in most other countries. To a large extent, the balance of payments deficits were, in fact, caused by the inflation; and, more important, the single remedy of reducing the pressure of internal demand in the deficit countries has helped solve both the internal and the external imbalance, as in Britain in 1955-8. It has not been necessary to face up to the dilemma implicit in the gold standard, that correction of external disequilibrium may cause internal disequilibrium.

Sooner or later, however, it will be necessary to face up to this dilemma and make more explicit decisions about the form of the international payments system used to replace the discriminatory system. Disturbances are always affecting the world economy, and it is extremely unlikely that balance of payments equilibrium between countries can be maintained indefinitely simply by maintaining internal balance within each country. Even if every country is able to maintain internal price stability with full employment (and it is doubtful whether this can be done, all the time) balance of payments disequilibrium between individual countries and the rest of the world is almost certain to develop, unless deliberate policies are used to prevent this happening.

One way in which this imbalance can develop is as a result of a change in tastes from the goods of one country towards those of another. Probably more important are the changes that are likely to occur over time as a result of differing rises in productivity which lead to differing rises in real incomes in different countries. If productivity is rising relatively fast at home, real incomes must also be rising relatively fast at home, if full employment is being maintained. On the other hand, if productivity is rising slowly abroad, real incomes there rise slowly. Now, if both the home and the foreign country spend the same proportion of this additional real income on imports from the other country, the consequence will be that the home country's imports tend to rise faster than the foreign country's imports, so that the home country moves into balance of payments deficit as a result of the faster rises in productivity and real income there. But this is not the whole story—there is no reason why the two countries should spend the same proportions of this additional real income on imports. For example, the rapid rise in productivity at home may be in industries closely competitive with imports, so that a relatively small proportion of the associated rise in real income goes to imports. Thus the balance of payments between two countries may move either way, if productivity is rising at different speeds in the two countries and even if they both contrive to maintain internal balance. The important thing is that the balance of payments is most unlikely to remain unchanged in these circumstances. Since productivity almost inevitably does rise at different speeds in different countries, some mechanism for bringing about balance of payments adjustment is almost certainly necessary, even in the unlikely event of each country in the world maintaining a high degree of internal balance.

Sooner or later, therefore, it is likely that a decision will have to be taken whether to resolve a dilemma of choice between internal and external balance, either by exchange rate changes or by controls; and in turn the former choice might involve step changes as in the I.M.F. or flexible rates, while the latter might involve either discriminatory or non-discriminatory methods.

This discussion of post-war international monetary experience inevitably ends on an uncertain note, because we are in a period of transition. What international adjustment mechanisms will come to be used in future is uncertain; but what is certain is that a satisfactory mechanism is likely to demand a high degree of internal equilibrium in the various countries, combined with absorption of temporary balance of payments disturbances by changes in reserves, and appropriate use of one or more of the other methods of adjustment, namely the use of exchange rate changes, of changes in the degree of use of controls, and changes in flows of long-term capital. What is more, it is clear that no purely automatic system is adequate to achieve satisfactory international adjustment; we shall have to rely on delicate and conscious control.

Appendix

SPECIMEN BALANCE SHEETS

BANK OF ENGLAND
28th February, 1958

ISSUE DEPARTMENT

Asseb

					£
Notes Issued—					
In Circulation	...	...	...	1,965,617,998
In Banking Department	...	...	...	34,740,863

£2,000,358,861

Liabs.

					£
Government Debt	...	...	...	11,015,100
Other Government Securities	...	...	...	1,985,214,175
Other Securities ...	...	...	...	755,987
Coin other than Gold Coin ...	...	...	...	3,014,738
Amount of Fiduciary Issue ...	...	...	...	£2,000,000,000
Gold Coin and Bullion (at 249s. 5d. per oz. fine) ...				358,861

£2,000,358,861

L. K. O'BRIEN,
Chief Cashier.

BANKING DEPARTMEMT

Liab

						£
Capital ...	...	...	...	...	...	14,553,000
Rest	...	...	...	...	...	3,914,472
Public Deposits (including Exchequer, Savings Banks, Commissioners of National Debt, and Dividend Accounts) ...			...	...	...	10,947,186
Other Deposits—						
Bankers ...	...	...	...	£232,160,401	
Other Accounts ...	...	...	£74,189,318		

306,349,719

£335,764,377

assets

					£
Government Securities	...	...	...	...	253,929,862
Other Securities—					
Discounts and Advances	...	£23,215,010		
Securities ...	...	£21,532,516		
					44,747,526
Notes	...	...	...	...	34,740,863
Coin	...	...	...	...	2,346,126

£335,764,377

L. K. O'BRIEN,
Chief Cashier.

LONDON CLEARING BANKS
December 31st, 1957

						£ million
Current accounts	...	...	...	...	...	4,192
Deposit accounts	...	...	...	...	...	2,737
Total deposits	...	...	...	...	...	£6,929

ASSETS

	£ million	Per cent. of total deposits	
Coin, notes and balances with Bank of England	... ...	601	8·7
Money at call or short notice	... ...	525	7·6
Bills discounted	... ...	1 538	22·2
Investments	... ...	2,049	29·6
Advances	... ...	1,881	27·1
Total of above assets	... ...	£6,594	

38·5 liquid assets

earning assets.

NOTE: Liabilities and assets do not balance because certain minor items are excluded in the consolidation.

A LIST OF BOOKS FOR FURTHER READING

THE following are among the books and articles which will be found most useful by anyone who wishes to read more about the subject matter of this book.

General

Among general economics textbooks which treat the economics of income and money in adequate detail are:

P. A. Samuelson: *Economics—an Introductory Analysis*, 4th edition.

W. J. Baumol and L. V. Chandler: *Economic Processes and Policies*.

At a more elementary level, G. Crowther's *Outline of Money* is still useful, although in some respects it is definitely dated.

Intermediate in level between this book and the author's *Outline of Monetary Economics* is J. H. B. Tew's very useful *Wealth and Income* (particularly the new second edition).

Income (*Chapter 2*)

A very useful introduction to national income accounting is

J. E. Meade and J. R. N. Stone: *National Income and Expenditure*.

At a more advanced level, use might be made of

H. C. Edey and A. T. Peacock: *National Income and Social Accounting*, and

R. L. Marris: *Political Arithmetic*.

The Levels of Income, Activity and Output (*Chapter 3*)

The fundamental statement of the modern theory of

income determination is to be found in the most important economics book of the first half of the twentieth century, namely

J. M. Keynes: *The General Theory of Employment, Interest and Money.*

Some readers will find A. H. Hansen's *A Guide to Keynes* a useful guide to the study of a fairly difficult book—and to the bitter controversies it aroused. Some of these can be traced by the curious in three of the sets of readings published by the American Economic Association—*Readings in Monetary Theory*, *Readings in the Theory of Income Distribution* and *Readings in Business Cycle Theory*. Also useful as a guide to the Keynesian Revolution is S. E. Harris (editor), *The New Economics.*

The Price Level (*Chapter 4*)

Despite a great deal of discussion, the theory of inflation has still not been particularly well developed by economists. Most useful are:

A. J. Brown: *The Great Inflation*

J. M. Keynes: *How to Pay for the War*

and an article in the *Economic Journal* for 1951 by R. Turvey called 'The Theory of Inflation in a Closed Economy'.

Economic Stabilization (*Chapter 5*)

J. R. Hicks: *A Contribution to the Theory of the Trade Cycle*

E. Lundberg and A. D. Knox (editors): *The Trade Cycle in the Post-War World.*

The Rate of Interest (*Chapter 6*)

Apart from the Keynesian literature mentioned in the section on the levels of income, output, and activity, D. H. Robertson's *Money* is important, and emphasizes a different point of view from the Keynesian literature.

Banking and the British Financial System (Chapters 7–9)

 R. S. Sayers: *Modern Banking*, 4th edition.

 Report of the Committee on Finance and Industry (The Macmillan Committee), Cmnd. 3897 of 1931.

 Report of the Committee on the Working of the Monetary System (The Radcliffe Committee), Cmnd. 827 of 1959.

The Theory of the Balance of Payments, etc. (Chapters 10–14)

A useful introduction from a rather different view-point from that followed in the text is J. Viner's *International Trade and Economic Development*.

Part I of J. H. B. Tew's *International Monetary Co-operation* is also useful. At a more advanced level, the standard works include:

 J. E. Meade: *The Balance of Payments*

 American Economic Association: *Readings in the Theory of International Trade.*

International Monetary Experience (Chapters 15–16)

A League of Nations Publication called *International Currency Experience* (catalogue II Econ. and Financial 1944. II A.4) is a valuable description of interwar experience. At a less advanced level, there is W. A. Lewis: *Economic Survey, 1919–39*.

On post-war experience, the third edition of J. H. B. Tew's *International Monetary Co-operation* is a good introduction, to be followed by R. Triffin's *Europe and the Money Muddle*, whose coverage is in fact much wider than Europe, and his more recent *Gold and the Dollar Crisis*.

INDEX

Printed in Great Britain by
The Camelot Press Ltd., London and Southampton